National Standards Curriculum Edition

Primary
Mathematics
for Jamaica

GRADE 2

Author
Elsa Segree-Royal

Lead Advisor
Lorna Thompson

Series Editor
Paul Broadbent

HODDER
EDUCATION
AN HACHETTE UK COMPANY

The Publishers would like to thank the following for permission to reproduce copyright material.

Photo credits

Acknowledgements

Every effort has been made to trace all copyright holders, but if any have been inadvertently overlooked, the Publishers will be pleased to make the necessary arrangements at the first opportunity.

Although every effort has been made to ensure that website addresses are correct at time of going to press, Hodder Education cannot be held responsible for the content of any website mentioned in this book. It is sometimes possible to find a relocated web page by typing in the address of the home page for a website in the URL window of your browser.

Hachette UK's policy is to use papers that are natural, renewable and recyclable products and made from wood grown in sustainable forests. The logging and manufacturing processes are expected to conform to the environmental regulations of the country of origin.

Orders: please contact Bookpoint Ltd, 130 Park Drive, Milton Park, Abingdon, Oxon OX14 4SE. Telephone: (44) 01235 827720. Fax: (44) 01235 400454. Email education@bookpoint.co.uk. Lines are open from 9 a.m. to 5 p.m., Monday to Saturday, with a 24-hour message answering service. You can also order through our website: www.hoddereducation.com

ISBN: 978 1 5104 0045 0

Illustrations by Oxford Designers and Illustrators Ltd
Typeset in India by Aptara Inc.
Printed in TK

A catalogue record for this title is available from the British Library.

Contents

Using this book

For the Students

Mathematics is all around us, with important skills and knowledge that you will use in your everyday life. It is also an amazing and interesting subject for you to enjoy. This textbook will help you master the different areas of mathematics, with activities and exercises to support your learning and give you practice.

Most importantly, the book will also encourage you to **think** like a mathematician! There are lots of problem-solving activities that will challenge you. This is great as you should be asking questions as well as answering them and spending time exploring the mathematics.

Mathematics is creative, so make sure you look for patterns, investigate and talk about the activities. It is also good to work together and support each other to solve problems.

We hope you enjoy working with this course!

- Your teacher will use the **Explain** boxes to help your understanding, so read these carefully and work through the examples.

- The **Remember** boxes are small reminders to give you advice and jog your memory.

- **Try this** activities will extend the mathematics or use it in a different way

- The **Reasoning** activities will need you to think carefully and explain what you are doing and why you are doing it. These may not all have a single answer, so explore, work with others and be creative.

For the Teachers

This mathematics series is intended to be used as a teaching and learning tool to support you with your planning and teaching and to give your students a rich variety of activities to help them master skills, concepts and procedures. It has been written and revised by Jamaican educators in line with Jamaica's National Standards Curriculum (NSC), with the structure and format of the series aiming to develop a depth of understanding through its careful progression.

The approach is in-line with current thinking on the teaching of mathematics, with an emphasis on the 21st Century Skills of critical thinking, creativity, collaboration and communication.

Critical thinking
Opportunities for reasoning, problem-solving and strategic thinking are essential in helping students develop a depth of understanding of mathematical ideas and concepts. Reasoning activities shown by the <> logo encourage critical thinking, with problems to solve and questions that ask students to show their reasoning and explain their results.

Creativity
Mathematics is a creative subject and, wherever appropriate, this series includes opportunities to explore, build, investigate, design and link to other areas of the curriculum. References and examples are also reflective of the Jamaican experience to show mathematics used in everyday situations.

Collaboration
Pairs or small groups of students are encouraged to collaborate to help each other solve the problems in the **Try this** and **Reasoning** activities. There are also opportunities to work together as a class through the **Explain** activities, discussing the examples and explanation shown.

Communication
Students can explain what they are doing and why they are doing it, through probing questioning. Questions should allow students to talk, explain and show their understanding and reasoning, for example: *'What do you notice?'*, *'Can you see a pattern?'*, *'What have you discovered?'*, *'How did you find that out?'*, *'Why do you think that?'*, *'Can you explain your reasoning?'*

The wide range of activities within the textbooks also reflect **Webb's Depth of Knowledge** model. The 4 DOK levels are not sequential or developmental, but it is important that students have a broad experience of all the levels to gain a deep understanding of the mathematics:

DOK-1 Recall and reproduction
DOK-2 Basic application of skills and concepts
DOK-3 Strategic thinking
DOK-4 Extended thinking

The activities shown by the <> **logo** have a particular Level 3 focus and require reasoning and higher order thinking skills than Level 1 and 2 activities. There are also **Extended Projects** each term that give opportunities for Level 4 extended thinking.

Formative assessment is an important part of teaching and learning, checking that students have a good understanding of concepts and skills before moving on with the learning. **Assess and Review** questions are also provided in the textbooks to give teachers the opportunity to evaluate the progress of the students.

1 Numbers

Comparing sets

Explain

A **set** is a group of objects.
These baskets show two sets of fruit.

Some sets have the same amount and some have more or less. Compare these baskets. Which has more fruit?

We use > , < or = to compare sets.

> means **is greater than**

< means **is less than**

= means **is equal to**

1 Compare the sets and write >, < or = to complete these.

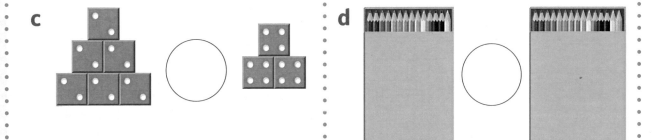

Reasoning activity

Write < and > on two pieces of paper. **Work in pairs** and each take a handful of counters. Count them aloud and place < or > between the two sets to make it true.

Colour the same

1 Tick the set with the matching number of items.

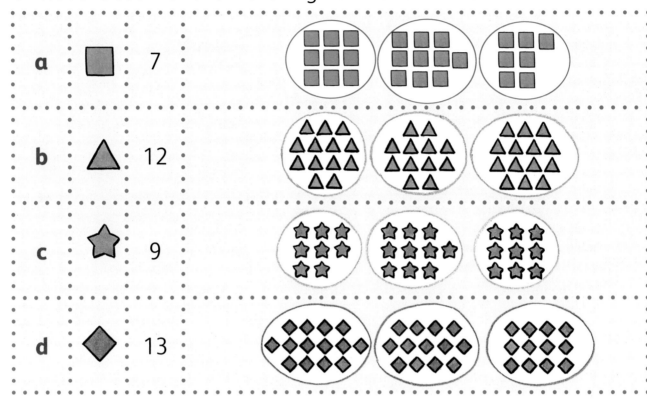

a	▢	7
b	△	12
c	☆	9
d	◆	13

2 Colour the set with the matching amount in coins.

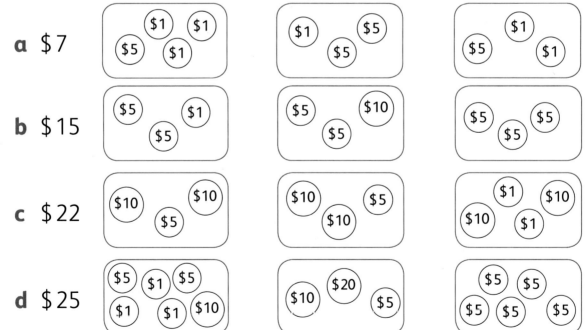

a $7

b $15

c $22

d $25

Try this

Work in pairs and use coins to make an amount of money more than $10.
Can each of you make the same amount, but with different coins?

Making tens and ones

11 ones make 1 ten and 1 one.

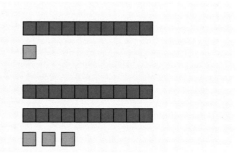

23 ones make 2 tens and 3 ones.

1 Complete the table.

Number	Tens	Ones
25	2	5
20	____	____
1	____	____

Number	Tens	Ones
8	____	____
24	____	____
2	____	____

2 Fill in the missing numbers.

a 11 = 10 + ____ = ____ ten and ____ one

b 22 = 10 + ____ + ____ = ____ tens and ____ ones

c ____ = 10 + 10 + 9 = ____ tens and ____ ones

d ____ = 10 + 10 + 5 = ____ tens and ____ ones

e ____ = ____ + ____ + ____ = 2 tens and 7 ones

3 Complete the number sentences.

a 27 = 20 + 7   **b** 25 = ____ + ____

c 18 = ____ + ____   **d** 19 = ____ + ____

e 13 = ____ + ____   **f** 10 + 4 = ____

g 24 = ____ + ____   **h** 20 + 6 = ____

i 26 = ____ + ____   **j** ____ + ____ = 17

k 21 = ____ + ____   **l** ____ + ____ = 14

Reasoning activity

Use linking cubes or counters to show these two numbers as tens and ones.

35   53

How are the digits 3 and 5 different in each number?

Ordering 2-digit numbers

Explain

We often need to put numbers in order of size.
Compare the tens and then the ones to help put them in order.

1 Write the house numbers in the correct order from smallest to largest.

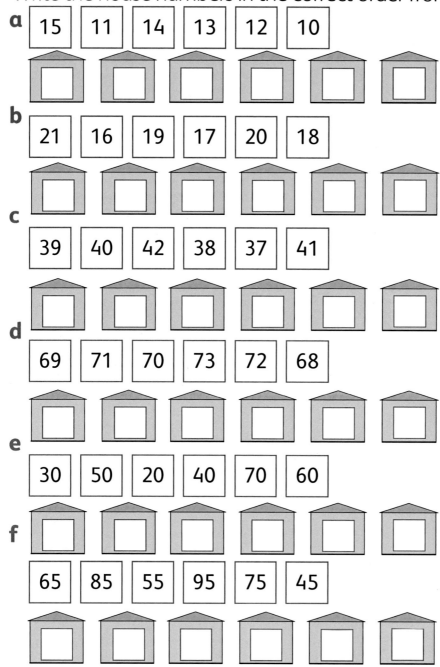

a | 15 | 11 | 14 | 13 | 12 | 10

b | 21 | 16 | 19 | 17 | 20 | 18

c | 39 | 40 | 42 | 38 | 37 | 41

d | 69 | 71 | 70 | 73 | 72 | 68

e | 30 | 50 | 20 | 40 | 70 | 60

f | 65 | 85 | 55 | 95 | 75 | 45

Try this

Work in groups and think of real life situations where numbers are placed in order.

Place value to 999

These blocks represent numbers. | 100 | | 10 | | 1 |

1 Fill in the hundreds, tens and ones.

a 100 100 10 10 1 1 1 1 1

H	T	O
2	2	5

b 100 100 100 100 100
10 10 10 10 10 1

H	T	O

c 100 100 100 100 1 1 1 1 1
1 1 1 1
10 10 10

H	T	O

d 100 100 100 100 1 1 1
1 1 1
100 100 100 100 100 1 1 1

H	T	O

e 100 10 1 1 1
1 1 1
1 1 1

H	T	O

f 100 100 10 10 10 10 10 1 1 1
10 10 10 10

H	T	O

g 100 100 100 10 10 1 1
100 100 100 10 10 1 1 1

H	T	O

Try this

Try counting on from different numbers. How much farther can you count if you begin at 99? Now count on from each answer above.

5

Working with numbers to 999

Explain

We can write numbers in **figures** or **words**.

① ① ①
① ①
① ①

7

seven

10 ① ① ①
① ①
10 ① ①

27

twenty-seven

100 10 ① ①
100 10 ①
100 10 ① ①

235

two hundred and thirty-five

1 Write the number in figures and in words.

a
① ① ①
① ① ①
① ① ①

_____

_____

b
10 10 10
10 10

_____

_____

c
10 10 10 10
① ① ① ① ① ①

_____

_____

d
100 100 100 10 ①
①
100 100 100 10 ①
①
100 100 10 10 ①
①

_____

_____

e
100 100 100

_____

_____

f
10 10 10 10

_____

_____

g
100 100 100
100 100 100 ①
①
100 10 10 ①

_____

_____

h
100 100 100 100 10
10 10 10 10 10
10 10 10 ① ①
① ① ① ① ① ①

_____

_____

i
100 100 100
① ① ① ①
① ① ① ①

_____

_____

Try this

Use $10 coins and $100 notes and count in tens and in hundreds.

Hundreds, tens and ones

1 How many?

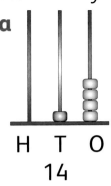
H   T   O
14

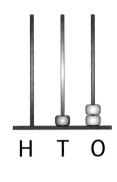
H   T   O
_____

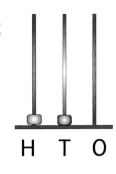
H   T   O
_____

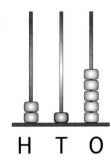
H   T   O
_____

2 Draw beads on the rods to show the number.

H   T   O
17

H   T   O
100

H   T   O
191

H   T   O
135

3 Complete the number sentences.

a $100 + 10 +$ _____ $= 112$ b $138 = 100 +$ _____ $+ 8$
c $200 +$ _____ $+ 6 = 256$ d $215 =$ _____ $+ 10 + 5$
e _____ $+ 20 + 6 = 326$ f $392 = 300 +$ _____ $+ 2$
g $400 +$ _____ $+ 7 = 457$

4 Fill in the missing numbers.

a

100 ___ 102 ___ ___ ___ ___ 107 ___ ___ 110

b
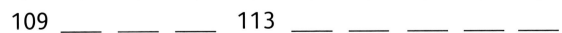
109 ___ ___ ___ 113 ___ ___ ___ ___ ___ 119

Reasoning activity

Start at 327 and count on in 10s. Start again and count on in 100s.
Draw beads on rods to help you. What do you notice?

Comparing 3-digit numbers

1 Fill in < or >.

    a 108 ◯ 103   **b** 125 ◯ 135

    c 256 ◯ 356   **d** 671 ◯ 299

    e 500 ◯ 408   **f** 932 ◯ 735

Reasoning activity

How did you work out your answers to question 1? How did you use hundreds, tens and ones to help you compare two 3-digit numbers? **In pairs,** discuss the steps to follow to work out which number is bigger.

2 Now use the same method to order these numbers. Write each set in order from smallest to greatest.

    a 998   908   980   999

    ____   ____   ____   ____

    b 754   647   832   599

    ____   ____   ____   ____

    c 562   429   964   256

    ____   ____   ____   ____

    d 747   474   774   714

    ____   ____   ____   ____

    e 919   945   594   199

    ____   ____   ____   ____

Remember

To compare numbers, look at the digit with the greatest value first: hundreds, then tens, then ones. To help write each digit under the headings H T O.

At the library

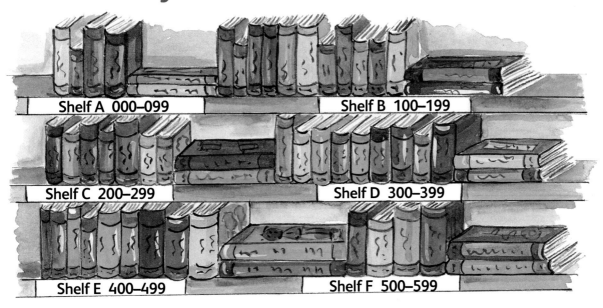

Shelf A 000–099   Shelf B 100–199
Shelf C 200–299   Shelf D 300–399
Shelf E 400–499   Shelf F 500–599

1 On which shelves would the librarian put these books?
Write the number and the shelf letter.

____   Shelf ____   ____   Shelf ____

____   Shelf ____   ____   Shelf ____

____   Shelf ____   ____   Shelf ____

2 Order these numbers from smallest to largest.

  a 235 852 731 963 257   ___ ___ ___ ___ ___

  b 127 837 351 764 219   ___ ___ ___ ___ ___

3 Underline the heavier mass in each pair.

  a 70g   84g   **b** 520kg   250kg   **c** 560kg 506kg

  d 190g 901g   **e** 237kg 327kg   **f** 600g 599g

Reasoning activity

Is a number with 3 digits always bigger than a number with 2 digits?
How can you prove this?

9

Comparing larger numbers

Which book in each pair has more pages? Fill in < or >.

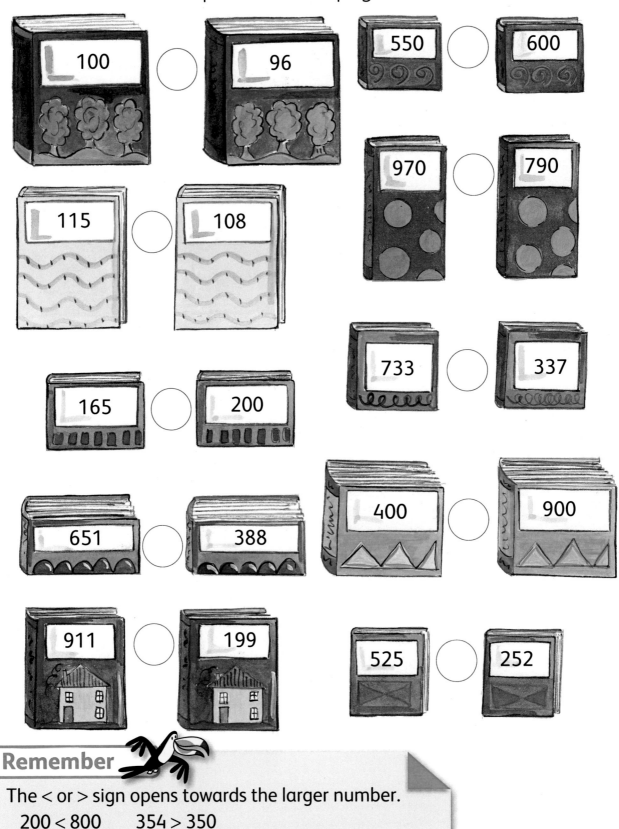

2 Time and length

Days of the week

1 Number these days in order starting with Sunday.

Monday
Wednesday
Tuesday   Friday
Sunday
Thursday   Saturday

2 Complete the sentences.

   a Today is _____.

   b Tomorrow will be _____.

   c Yesterday was _____.

   d The day after tomorrow will be _____.

   e There are _____ days in one week.

   f My favourite day of the week is _____.

Try this

Ask 10 friends what day of the week is their favourite.
Show their answers on the graph. Shade one block for each person.

Sunday	Monday	Tuesday	Wednesday	Thursday	Friday	Saturday

   a Which day do most of your friends like best?

   b Which day did fewest friends choose?

Time

1 Complete the table.

If today is:	Tomorrow will be	In two days' time it will be	Yesterday was	A week from today it will be
Tuesday				
Thursday				
Saturday				
Monday				

2 Use this calendar to complete the sentences below.

July						
Sunday	Monday	Tuesday	Wednesday	Thursday	Friday	Saturday
		1	2	3	4	5
6	7	8	9	10	11	12
13	14	15	16	17	18	19
20	21	22	23	24	25	26
27	28	29	30	31		

a July 8th was a _____.

b July 16th was a _____.

c The day and date five days before July 20th was a

_____ July_____.

d The last day of June was _____.

e The August 1st will be on a _____.

f 10 days after Sunday July 13th was July _____.

Try this

Work in pairs and use a wall calendar and find the following:
- What date did we start this term?
- When do school holidays start?
- Find the first/last day of each month.
- Can you find your birthday?

Collecting data

1 Fill in your own name and birthday in the table.

2 Fill in when five others have their birthdays.

3 Use a calendar for this year to find out on what day each birthday falls. Write the days in the third column.

Name	Birthday	Day of birthday

Make a birthday card for a friend

You need: a sheet of plain paper and crayons.

☆ Fold the sheet of paper in half.

☆ Draw stars on the front of the card to show the age of your friend.

☆ Write *Happy Birthday* inside.

☆ Use the information from the table and write the date and day of their birthday.

Try this

Your birthday will not fall on the same day of the week every year. Look at a calendar for last year. What day was your birthday?

Reasoning activity

Look at online calendars and find the day of the week you were born for each year, in order. What do you notice about the days?

Months

1 Match the parts to make the names of the months.

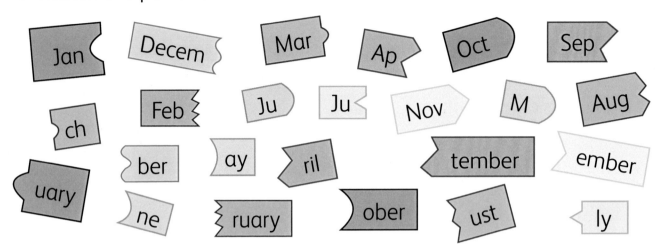

2 Write the names in order from the 1st to the 12th.

1st month	_____	7th month	_____
2nd month	_____	8th month	_____
3rd month	_____	9th month	_____
4th month	_____	10th month	_____
5th month	_____	11th month	_____
6th month	_____	12th month	_____

3 Complete the sentences.

a Christmas is in _____. This is the _____ month.

b October comes after _____. October is the _____ month.

c _____ has the fewest days of all the months – only 28.

d July and _____ are months with four letters in their names.

e My birthday is in _____, the _____ month.

Remember

The number of a month is used when writing dates: 24th December 2018 is written 24/12/18.

Comparing lengths

1 Put ✗ on the shortest in each set.
Put ✔ on the longest in each set.

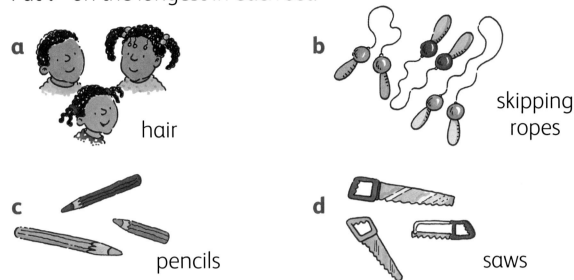

a hair

b skipping ropes

c pencils

d saws

2 Write **T** next to the tallest object in each set.
Write **S** next to the shortest object in each set.

a

b

c

Try this

What is the tallest building you have seen?
Where is this building?

Remember

To compare lengths of real things, use the words *shorter* and *longer*,
shortest and *longest*, *taller* and *tallest*.

Units of length

Reasoning activity

Use your handspan to measure the length of your desk.

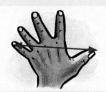 = 1 handspan

Did everyone in your class get the same answer?
Why or why not?

Explain

To measure exactly, we use standard units of length: **metres** (m), **centimetres** (cm) and **kilometres** (km).

100 centimetres = 1 metre

1000 metres = 1 kilometre   ⊢——⊣   1 cm

1 Which unit would you use? Write m, cm or km.

a
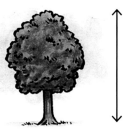

b
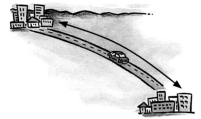

c

d

Reasoning activity

Why do you think we measure with centimetres and metres rather than a handspan?

16

3 Shapes and paths

Paths

A **path** is a set of points with two end points. The path above starts at point A and ends at point K. A **straight line** is the shortest (most direct) path between two points, like this: A ●————————● B

Here are some more paths:

curved path

straight path

closed path

1 Draw the most direct path between each pair of points.

a P Q

b
● F

● G

c
● J

● K

2 Complete the unfinished path in each pair so that the paths cross.

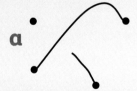

a

b

c

3 Close each path by drawing along the dotted lines.

a

b

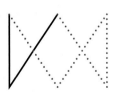

c

Work in groups and find examples of straight and curved paths in real life. Look at the edges of windows, walls and floors, and at rivers and roads on maps.

Closed paths

1 Join the dots to make each closed path.
Write the name of the shape you have formed.

a

_____

b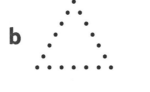

_____

c

_____

d

_____

e

_____

f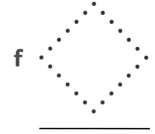

_____

2 a Colour red the shape with three straight sides.

  b Colour yellow the other shapes that have only straight sides.

  c Colour green the remaining shapes.

3 a How many shapes did you colour yellow? _____

  b How many shapes did you colour green? _____

4 Circle the closed paths below.

    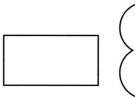

Reasoning activity

Work in pairs and write the letters of the alphabet in these sets:
curved path   straight path   closed path
Which letters were difficult to put into these groups? Why?

Circles, triangles and squares

Circles, triangles and squares are examples of closed shapes.

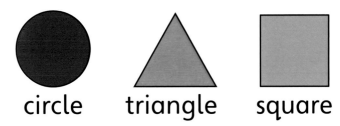

circle   triangle   square

1 Draw the missing sides to make triangles.

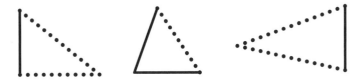

2 Draw the missing sides to make squares.

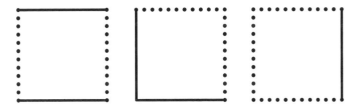

3 Draw circles to complete the pattern.

Make up your own patterns using these shapes.

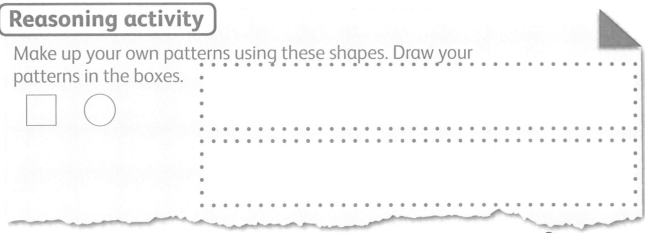

Reasoning activity

Make up your own patterns using these shapes. Draw your
patterns in the boxes.

Assess and review

I can read and write numbers to 999, read a calendar, know some standard units of length and explore paths and shapes.

1 Complete each number sentence and write the numbers in words. Draw beads on the rods to show the number.

H   T   O

$200 + \_\_\_ + 6 = 256$

_____

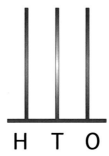

H   T   O

$\_\_\_ + 10 + \_\_\_ = 415$

_____

2 Write the missing months from this calendar.

January	February		April
May		July	August
	October	November	

3 Circle the unit you would use to measure the length of the calendar above:

metres   centimetres   kilometres

4 Join these dots with a straight lines.

What shape have you drawn? _____

4 3-digit numbers

Expanded notation

Explain

You know how to write numbers as hundreds, tens and ones.

For example:

459 = 4 hundreds + 5 tens + 9 ones

or 459 = 400 + 50 + 9

This is called **expanded notation**.

The position of each digit in the
number helps us to work out its value.

H	T	O
3	8	5

3̲85   The 3 represents 300.

3_8_5   The 8 represents 80.

38_5_   The 5 represents 5.

1 Write the value of the underlined digit in each number in words
   and in numbers. The first one has been done for you.

   a 4_5_6 _____fifty_____   __50__

   b _9_72 _____   ____

   c 10_5_ _____   ____

   d 9_3_4 _____   ____

2 Write these number in expanded notation. Write your answers
   as numerals, not words. The first one has been done for you.

   a 187 __100 + 80 + 7__   b 470 _____

   c 96   _____   d 288 _____

   e 100 _____   f 447 _____

Remember

Reading each number aloud will help you
find the value of each digit.

Hundreds, tens and ones

Explain

258 = 2 hundreds 5 tens 8 ones

H	T	O
2	5	8

1 Write whether the underlined digit represents hundreds, tens or ones. The first one has been done for you.

   a 4<u>9</u>9 ___hundreds___   b 54<u>2</u> _____

   c 3<u>6</u>5 _____   d 78<u>0</u> _____

   e <u>4</u>3 _____   f <u>2</u>76 _____

2 Write how many hundreds, tens and ones.

		Hundreds	Tens	Ones
a	678	6	7	8
b	432	___	___	___
c	126	___	___	___
d	101	___	___	___
e	950	___	___	___
f	555	___	___	___

Reasoning activity

How many different 3-digit numbers can you make using 5, 3 and 8?
What is the largest number you can make? What is the smallest?
How do you know they are the largest and smallest numbers?

Ordering 3-digit numbers

We can put numbers in order from smallest to largest or from largest to smallest.

Example

A group of friends were bird-watching. David counted 102 birds, Matthew counted 120 birds and Helen counted 107 birds.

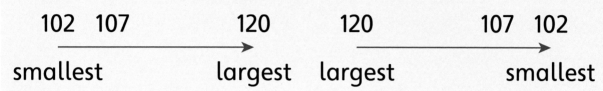

102   107   120   120   107   102

smallest   largest   largest   smallest

1   Put these numbers in order from smallest to largest.
    Use the number line to help.

    142   132   152   172   162   192   202   182   212

    ___   ___   ___   ___   ___   ___   ___   ___   ___

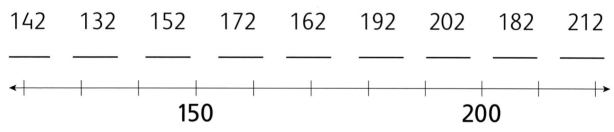

                    150   200

2   Circle the larger number in each pair.
    a 105   150   b 200   215   c 280   218
    d 165   166   e 146   144   f 358   258
    g 110   210   h 130   310

3   Write these numbers in order from largest to smallest.

    300   700
              150
                        largest ___ ___ ___ smallest
    900   859

Reasoning activity

How does a number line help you put numbers in order?
Explain and show this to a classmate.

23

Counting in 2s and 3s

1 Start on 2. Count in 2s. Colour every second number.

1	2	3	4	5	6	7	8	9	10
11	12	13	14	15	16	17	18	19	20

2 Count in 3s. Write the numbers that you land on.

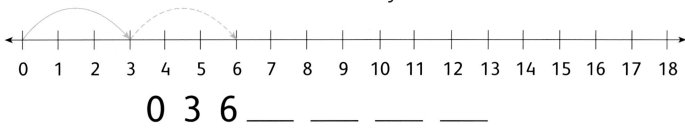

0 3 6 ___ ___ ___ ___

3 How many legs? Count and write the total.

Counting in 3s and 4s

1 Count in 3s. Circle every third number.
The first one has been done for you.

1	2	③	4	5	6	7	8	9	10
11	12	13	14	15	16	17	18	19	20
21	22	23	24	25	26	27	28	29	30

2 Go up the steps 4 at a time. Colour each fourth step.
The first one has been done for you.

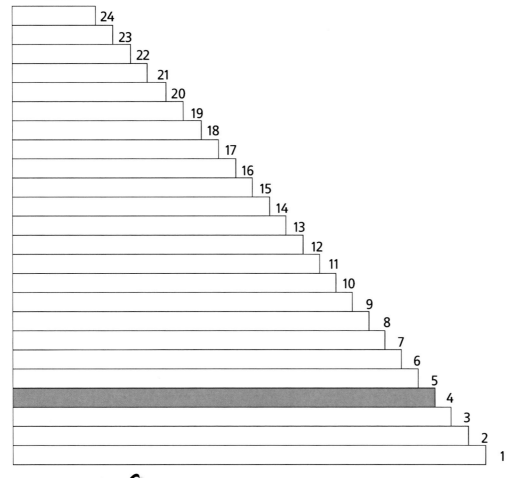

Finish!

Count chair legs in 4s. How many are there in
your classroom? Now count table legs in 4s.

Counting in 5s

1 Join the dots. Start with 5 and count in 5s.

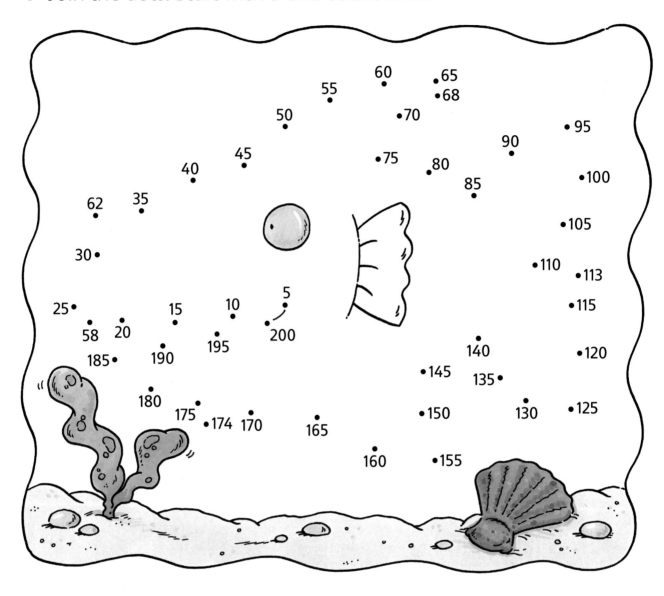

a What did you make? _____

b How many 5s did you join from 5 to 50? _____

c What number is halfway between 5 and 25? _____

d What number is 5 more than 30? _____

e How many 5s are there in 50? _____

Reasoning activity

Which numbers were left over on the picture? Why?

26

10s and 5s

1 Count in 10s and write how many.

  _____20_____

    _____

      _____

     _____

2 Use the hundred chart.

   a Count in 5s and colour all the answers blue.

   b Count in 10s and circle the answers.

Reasoning activity

What do you notice?

3 Fill in the missing numbers. Use the hundred chart to help you.

   a 5 10 ___ ___ 25 ___ ___

   b 40 ___ 50 ___ 60 ___ 70

   c 10 ___ 30 40 ___ ___ 70

1	2	3	4	5	6	7	8	9	10
11	12	13	14	15	16	17	18	19	20
21	22	23	24	25	26	27	28	29	30
31	32	33	34	35	36	37	38	39	40
41	42	43	44	45	46	47	48	49	50
51	52	53	54	55	56	57	58	59	60
61	62	63	64	65	66	67	68	69	70
71	72	73	74	75	76	77	78	79	80
81	82	83	84	85	86	87	88	89	90
91	92	93	94	95	96	97	98	99	100

4 Complete these.

   a 5 + 5 = ___   **b** 20 − 5 = ___   **c** 20 + 10 = ___

   d 10 + 5 = ___   **e** 35 − 5 = ___   **f** 50 + 40 = ___

   g 25 + 5 = ___   **h** 90 − 5 = ___   **i** 0 + 10 = ___

   j 0 + 5 = ___   **k** 100 − 5 = ___   **l** 20 − 10 = ___

   m 55 + 5 = ___   **n** 10 + 10 = ___   **o** 30 − 10 = ___

   p 10 − 5 = ___   **q** 40 + 10 = ___   **r** 95 − 10 = ___

Try this

How many fingers and toes are there in total in your class?
Did you count in 5s or 10s?

Counting in sequence

1 Fill in the missing numbers.

a Count in ones.

9			11	
18	19			
		30		
97				
		79		

b Count in fives.

5			15	
35			45	
75			85	
		25		
		55		

c Count in tens.

10			30	
40			60	
		80		
70				
30				

2 Circle the numbers in the right hand column that are:

> 11	9 13 20 10
< 32	20 23 35 30
> 12	(3 + 6) (4 + 7) (5 + 9) (6 + 7)
< 25	(10 + 5) (15 + 5) (25 − 5) (30 − 10)
< 60	59 61 67 65
> 89	88 87 90 99
> 15 and also < 20	13 16 19 25 12 14 23 17
> 5 and also < 15	3 7 9 17 2 6 10 14
> 24 and also < 42	22 33 44 55 25 28 34 45
> 30 and also < 60	25 35 45 55 65 33 56 63

Remember

> means 'is greater than' and < means 'is less than'.

Position

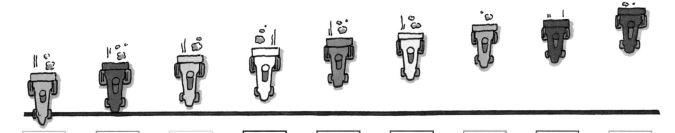

| 1 | 2 | 3 | 4 | 5 | 6 | 7 | 8 | 9 |

1 Underline the position in which each car finished the race.

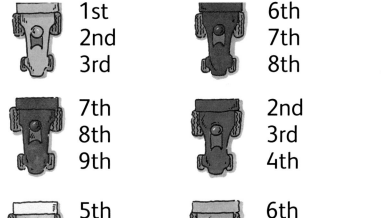

1st   6th   3rd
2nd   7th   4th
3rd   8th   5th

7th   2nd   4th
8th   3rd   5th
9th   4th   6th

5th   6th   3rd
6th   7th   4th
7th   8th   5th

2 a What day of the week is

the 12th? _____

the 25th? _____

b What day of the week is it seven days after

the 15th? _____

the 23rd? _____

Su	M	Tu	W	Th	F	S
Sunday	Monday	Tuesday	Wednesday	Thursday	Friday	Saturday
	1	2	3	4	5	6
7	8	9	10	11	12	13
14	15	16	17	18	19	20
21	22	23	24	25	26	27
28	29	30	31			

Reasoning activity

In groups stand in a line in height order.
Start with the shortest, who is 1st? 2nd? last? Now start with the tallest, who is 1st? 2nd? last?
What happened to the position of the tallest and shortest person?

29

5 Finding lengths

Centimetres

A **centimetre** is a unit of length. ⊢——⊣ = 1 cm

1 Estimate the height of each sunflower in centimetres (cm). Then use your ruler to measure.

a   b   c   d

Estimate: ____ ____ ____ ____

Measure: ____ ____ ____ ____

e   f   g   h

Estimate: ____ ____ ____ ____

Measure: ____ ____ ____ ____

Measuring lengths in metres

We use **metres** (m) to measure longer objects.
There are 100 centimetres in 1 metre.

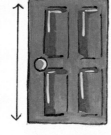

100 cm = 1 m

about 1 m   about 2 m

1   Estimate these measurements on real objects in metres.
    Use the lengths above to help you.

a _____ m   b _____ m   c _____ m

2   Which units would you use to measure the length of these?
    Fill in cm or m.

a   b   c   d   e

___   ___   ___   ___   ___

3   Which is longer? Underline the correct answers.
    a 1 metre   or   1 centimetre
    b 25 centimetres or   1 metre
    c 10 cm   or   1 metre
    d 2 metres   or   20 centimetres

Try this

Using a metre stick, measure objects in your
classroom such as desks and doors.

Measuring with strips

Explain

10 centimetres = 1 decimetre
This is a **decimetre strip**.

Cut strips of paper 10 cm long.

1 Measure using your decimetre strips. Then measure in cm.

a

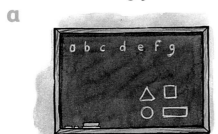

board length

_____ strips _____ cm

b

classroom length

_____ strips _____ cm

c

distance to the next classroom

_____ strips _____ cm

d

cupboard height

_____ strips _____ cm

Remember

A decimetre is not a common unit of
measurement, but it is useful for measuring
length between centimetres and metres.

Assess and review

I can put numbers in order, count in steps of 2, 3, 4, 5 and 10, use ordinal numbers and estimate and measure lengths.

1 Write these numbers in order from smallest to greatest.

784　　　　595　　　　　748　　　　　601　　　　　559

＿＿＿　　＿＿＿　　　＿＿＿　　　＿＿＿　　　＿＿＿

2 Write the missing numbers.

3 × 15 × 120

| 30 | | | 60 | 70 | 80 | |

| | 9 | 12 | | 18 | | 24 |

| 10 | | 20 | | 30 | 35 | |

3 Match the carriages to the positions.

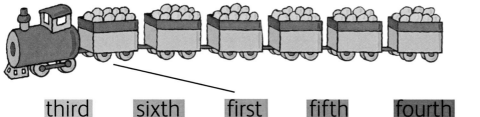

third　　　sixth　　　first　　　fifth　　　fourth　　　second

4 Estimate and measure the lengths of these ribbons.

Estimate: ＿＿＿　　Estimate: ＿＿＿
Measure: ＿＿＿　　Measure: ＿＿＿

Estimate: ＿＿＿
Measure: ＿＿＿

Adding and subtracting

Adding and subtracting

This number chart runs from 0 to 99.

It makes it easy to count on from any tens number.

What is 4 more than 30?

Start at 30 and count on 4 to 34.

You can also use it to count back to a tens number.

What is 47 subtract 7?

Start at 47 and count back 7 to 40.

The number chart shows columns of balloons numbered 9–99, 8–98, 7–97, 6–96, 5–95, 4–94, 3–93, 2–92, 1–91, 0–90.

1 Use the number chart to help you add these.

   a 20 + 8 = _____   b 30 + 5 = _____   c 40 + 2 = _____

   d 50 + 6 = _____   e 60 + 3 = _____   f 90 + 4 = _____

2 Use the number chart to help you subtract these.

   a 38 − 8 = _____   b 42 − 2 = _____   c 55 − 5 = _____

   d 61 − 1 = _____   e 79 − 9 = _____   f 87 − 7 = _____

Reasoning activity

Take away 9, then take away 10 from each 2-digit number in the top row of the number chart. What do you notice?

Do and undo

1 Do the addition. Then undo it. The first one has been done.

a

$\underline{9}$ – 2 = 7

7 + 2 = $\underline{9}$

b

6 – 1 = ____

5 + 1 = ____

c

____ – ____ = ____

6 + 2 = ____

d

____ – ____ = ____

15 + 6 = ____

2 Write + or – to complete these.

a 2 ◯ 3 = 5

b 5 ◯ 2 = 3

c 9 ◯ 2 = 7

d 4 ◯ 2 = 6

Try this

Write + or – and the missing numbers.

a 4 ◯ ____ = 8

b 9 ◯ ____ = 8

c ____ ◯ 4 = 8

d 7 ◯ 2 = 9

Remember

You can add in any order:

3 + 4 = 7   4 + 3 = 7

Subtraction

Explain

We can use groups of objects to subtract.

12 – 3 = 9   14 – 6 = 8

Do you notice that they are grouped in 5s to help you count and calculate?

1 Use the groups to help you subtract.

a   15 – 7 = ___      b   13 – 5 = ___

c   17 – 6 = ___   d   14 – 9 = ___

Try this

Use < , > or = to complete these.

a
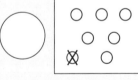

6 – 2   7 – 1

b
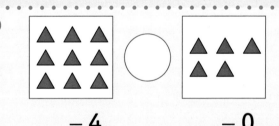

___ – 4   ___ – 0

c
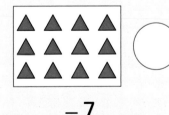

___ – 7   ___ – 8

d

___ – 2   ___ – 4

Subtraction problems

When you subtract, you:

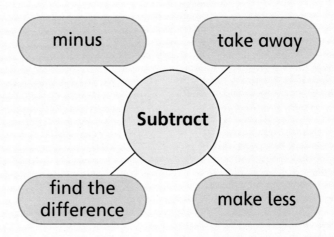

We can use a number line for subtraction.

What is 9 take away 3?   What is 19 – 17?
Count back like this   Count on like this

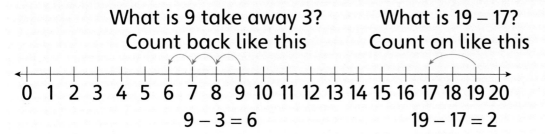

$$9 - 3 = 6 \qquad\qquad 19 - 17 = 2$$

1 Use the number line above to answer these.

a I had 12 marbles and I gave away 9.
How many marbles do I have left?

b Mum bought 14 oranges. 6 were spoilt and were thrown away.
How many of them does she now have?

c Sam lost 8 of his toy cars. He started with 17 cars.
How many has he got now?

d I have read 16 out of 20 pages of a magazine.
How many more pages do I have to read?

Reasoning activity

Use a number line to work out these subtractions.

a 11	**b** 13	**c** 35	**d** 17
-1	-3	-5	-7

What pattern do you notice?

7 How long?

Measuring lengths

The **metre** (m) is a unit we use to measure length.
Look at a metre stick to see how long it is.

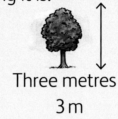

Three metres
3 m

1 Use a tape measure to measure these lengths.
   Write your answers in words and in numbers.

a

your classmate

_____

_____

b

your classroom door

_____

_____

c

a crayon

_____

_____

d

a cricket bat

_____

_____

e

a broom

_____

_____

f

a table leg

_____

_____

Reasoning activity

Work in pairs and group the objects by length. How have you grouped the objects? What groups did others use? Are they in the same way as you?

Estimating lengths

Use card to make a 10 cm snake strip.

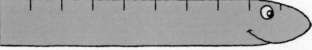

a Use your snake strip to estimate the length of different objects in the classroom and write your estimates in the table.

b Use a ruler to measure the same objects and write your results in the table.

I measured	My estimate (cm)	Actual length (cm)
height of a chair		
width of a door		
height of a class friend		
length of a desk		

1 Estimate the length of each line.

Measure each line using your ruler.

a ————————

Estimate: _____ cm

Length: _____ cm

b ——————————

Estimate: _____ cm

Length: _____ cm

c —————————

Estimate: _____ cm

Length: _____ cm

d ———————————————

Estimate: _____ cm

Length: _____ cm

Reasoning activity

Work in pairs, one of you measure these in centimetres and the other in metres. Can you calculate what your partner's measurements will be? Compare your answers to check.

• length of a desk = ____ m or ____ cm
• width of a door = ____ m or ____ cm
• height of a friend = ____ m or ____ cm

Units of measure

Explain

We measure length using **centimetres** (cm), **metres** (m) and **kilometres** (km).
1 km = 1000 m   1 m = 100 cm

1 Circle the unit you would use to measure each of these.

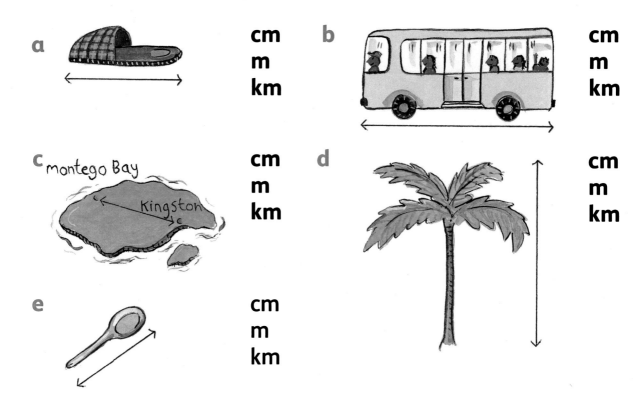

a   cm
      m
      km

b   cm
      m
      km

c montego Bay   cm
  Kingston   m
                   km

d   cm
      m
      km

e   cm
      m
      km

2 Write these in order of size from largest to smallest.

a 3 cm   3 km   3 m   _____ _____ _____

b 3 km   30 cm   10 m   _____ _____ _____

c 1 km   10 m   100 cm _____ _____ _____

Try this

$\frac{1}{2}$ metre is 50 cm. Try to improve your estimation skills
by estimating the lengths of different objects to the
nearest half of a metre. How close were your estimates?

8 Patterns and shapes

Making patterns

1 Draw the shapes to complete each pattern.

a

Shapes	Pattern

b

c

d

2 Now make your own patterns using these shapes.

a

Shapes	Pattern

b

c

Reasoning activity

In **pairs** take turns to draw a shape in one row, then repeat the pattern.

Rules and patterns

Explain

Look at this pattern and find the **rule**.

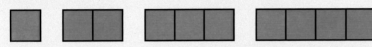

What does the next shape look like? What is the rule?
It is increasing by 1 square each time.

1 What comes next? Draw two more shapes for each pattern.

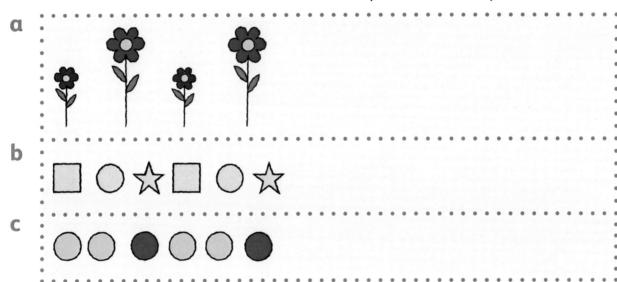

2 Continue these patterns.

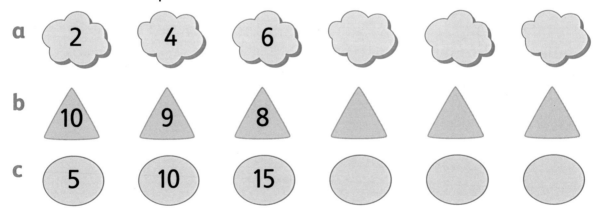

Reasoning activity

Work in pairs to find the rule and the next number for this number pattern.
1 2 4 8 16 ___

9 Showing information

Using graphs

Peter and Paula counted cars and bicycles. They made these graphs.

Peter's graph   **Paula's graph**

1 Use the graphs to find the answers.

   a Peter saw _____ bicycles.   **b** Paula saw _____ bicycles.

   c Peter saw _____ cars.   **d** Paula saw _____ cars.

   e Did Peter and Paula see the same cars and bicycles? _____

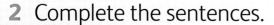

Reasoning activity

How are their graphs different?
Which graph do you prefer? Why?

2 Complete the sentences.

   a Peter drew a _____ graph.

   b Paula draw a _____ graph.

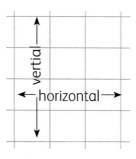

Remember

We arrange data in rows (lines across) and
columns (lines up and down).

Bar graphs

This is a picture of Kim's farm.

1 Count the animals.

a How many cows are there?

_____

b How many hens are there? _____

c How many dogs are there? _____

2 Fill in this information on the graph.
   Colour one block for each animal.

3 Look at your graph and write
   'more' or 'fewer' in each sentence.

a There are _____ hens than cows on the farm.

b There are _____ cows than dogs.

c There are _____ dogs than hens.

4 Answer these questions from your graph.

a Which animals are there most of? _____

b How many more cows are
   there than dogs? _____

c How many animals
   are there altogether on
   the farm? _____

Reasoning activity

Why do you think we show data
on a graph?
Could you have answered questions 3
and 4 as easily from the picture?

44

Working with data

'Leopards and elephants

Are foreign to me –

They inhabit places

Far across the sea.'

Tally tables

1 Count the vowels **a, e, i, o** and **u** in the poem above.

2 Make a tally mark like this / in the chart for each vowel that you count.
When you count five, cross the four previous tallies like this: ~~IIII~~

Vowel	Tally	Total
a		
e		
i		
o		
u		

3 Use this data to answer these.

   a Which vowel does not appear in the poem?_____

   b The vowel which appears most often is _____ .

   c Which vowel appears one more time than **i**? _____

Draw a bar graph to show this information.

Use the graph to answer question 3.

Did you find it easier to answer the questions using your graph, the tally
chart or the totals from question 2?

Assess and review

> I can add and subtract 1-digit numbers, measure in centimetres and metres, continue shape patterns and use tally charts.

1 Choose any two number cards.

| 17 | 9 | 22 | 5 |

Write an addition sentence with the numbers you chose.

_____ + _____ = _____

Choose two more numbers and write a subtraction sentence.

_____ – _____ = _____

2 Use a tape measure to measure these.
Write the lengths in metres or centimetres.

skipping rope

_____

width of the chalkboard

_____

3 Draw the next three for these patterns.

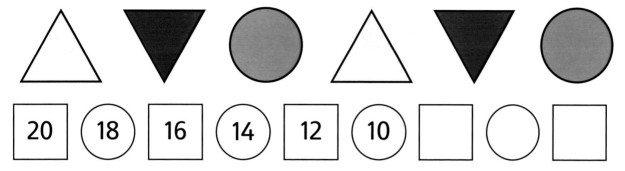

| 20 | 18 | 16 | 14 | 12 | 10 | | | |

4 These are the favourite colours of a class of children.
Write the total for each colour.

Colour	Tally	Total
Red	ⵏⵜ ///	
Blue	ⵏⵜ	
Green	ⵏⵜ /	
Orange	///	
Purple	////	

How many more children chose red than chose orange? _____

How many children were there in total in the class? _____

47

10 Addition and subtraction

Working with zero

1 Add zero.

a 7 + 0 = __7__ **b** 9 + 0 = _____ **c** 12 + 0 = _____

d 0 + 5 = _____ **e** 0 + 8 = _____ **f** 10 + 0 = _____

2 Subtract zero.

a 7 − 0 = __7__ **b** 9 − 0 = _____ **c** 12 − 0 = _____

d 16 − 0 = _____ **e** 5 − 0 = _____ **f** 10 − 0 = _____

> **Reasoning activity**
>
> What happens when you add or subtract zero?
>
> Why does this happen?
>
> Write a sentence explaining what zero means.

3 Make your own number sentences using zero.

a _____ + 0 = _____ **b** 0 + _____ = _____

c _____ − 0 = _____ **d** _____ − 0 = _____

4 Circle all the words that also mean zero.

none	everything	nil	nothing
some	all	empty set	nada
nought	one	a fraction	

> **Remember**
>
> Adding or subtracting zero does not change the total.
> Use counters to help you understand this idea.

Using a number line for subtraction

Explain

Mark has 10 mangoes. He eats 4.
How many are left?

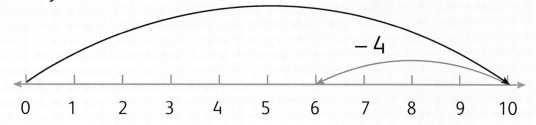

$10 - 4 = 6$
He has 6 mangoes left.

1 Use the number line above to help you subtract.

a $7 - 2 =$ _____   **b** $5 - 3 =$ _____   **c** $9 - 4 =$ _____

d $7 - 5 =$ _____   **e** $10 - 8 =$ _____   **f** $9 - 6 =$ _____

2 Use the 0–20 number line down the side of this page
to help you subtract.

a $19 - 3 =$ _____   **b** $20 - 7 =$ _____

c $14 - 3 =$ _____   **d** $11 - 4 =$ _____

e $17 - 5 =$ _____   **f** $16 - 11 =$ _____

Remember

To use a number line to subtract, jump forwards from the 0
to the starting number and count back.
For example, to subtract $12 - 4$, jump to 12 and count back 4 on
the number line to land on 8.

Subtraction practice

Explain

These are words that tell you to subtract.

We can use a number line to help us subtract.

(word web: subtract — less, left over, take away, subtract, difference between, lose, minus, remove, give away)

18 – 4

(number line from 0 to 18 showing an arc from 18 back to 14, labelled – 4)

0 1 2 3 4 5 6 7 8 9 10 11 12 13 14 15 16 17 18

18 – 4 = 14

1 Draw your own number line to help you work out these.

   a 19 – 5 = _____   **b** 10 – 9 = _____   **c** 20 – 8 = _____

   d 20 – 4 = _____   **e** 19 – 3 = _____   **f** 13 – 7 = _____

2 Use a number line to help you solve these problems.

   a Aneke's dog had 12 puppies. Aneke gave 9 to new owners. _____ puppies are left.

   b Mrs Martin had 25 desks in her classroom. 5 broke. _____ desks are left.

3 Solve these subtraction problems.

   a Take 18 from 28. _____ – _____ = _____

   b Subtract 10 from 20. _____ – _____ = _____

   c 27 minus 15 equals? _____ – _____ = _____

Reasoning activity

Draw your own vertical number line 0-20, with 20 at the top.

In pairs take turns to roll the dice and subtract that number on your number line. The first player to pass 1 is the winner.

Adding and subtracting tens

Explain

10	20	30	40	50	60	70	80	90	100
9	19	29	39	49	59	69	79	89	99
8	18	28	38	48	58	68	78	88	98
7	17	27	37	47	57	67	77	87	97
6	16	26	36	46	56	66	76	86	96
5	15	25	35	45	55	65	75	85	95
4	14	24	34	44	54	64	74	84	94
3	13	23	33	43	53	63	73	83	93
2	12	22	32	42	52	62	72	82	92
1	11	21	31	41	51	61	71	81	91

Each tower has 10 blocks. Use the towers to help you add and subtract in tens.

10 + 10 = _____

Point to 10 on the first tower. To add 1 more ten, move to the next column to the right. You are pointing at the answer. 10 + 10 = 20

90 – 30 = _____

Count each column from 10 to 90. These 9 tens tower together make 90.
To subtract 3 tens, move your finger three towers to the left. What do you see?

90 – 30 = 60

1 a 20 + 10 = _____ **b** 30 + 10 = _____

 c 40 + 30 = _____ **d** 50 + 50 = _____

2 a 30 – 10 = _____ **b** 40 – 20 = _____

 c 70 – 30 = _____ **d** 80 – 40 = _____

Remember

Read the tens numbers on the top of each tower in order from left to right.

Try this

Use $1 coins to make towers of ten coins.
How many towers of ten $1 coins do you need to make $40?
Make towers of ten $1 coins to make $70.
If you spend $50, how much would you have left?

Expand and add

Explain

20 +   12

= 10 + 10 + 10 + 2   Expand each number into tens and ones.

= 30 + 2   Add the tens together. Add the ones together.

= 32   Rename the number.

1 Rename these numbers using the method above.

a 30 + 19 =   **b** 40 + 16 =

_____   _____

_____   _____

_____   _____

c 50 + 17 =   **d** 60 + 15 =

_____   _____

_____   _____

_____   _____

e 70 + 11 =   **f** 80 + 12 =

_____   _____

_____   _____

_____   _____

Reasoning activity

Work in groups. Each pick a different teen number between 13-19.
Write the numbers 20-70 in order, in a column and add your teen number
to each of them.
What do notice about your answers and the answers of your group?
Repeat the task but subtract your teen number. What do you notice?

Problem solving

Explain

Sam has 12 crayons. He gets 4 more.
How many does he have altogether?

x = the total number of crayons

$x = 12 + 4$

$x = 16$

Sam has 16 crayons altogether.

You can use any letter or shape instead of x.

1 Use any shape or letter to solve each
problem.

a Kay had 6 tamarind balls. She gets 11 more.
How many does she have altogether?

_____ = the total number of tamarind balls

_____ = _____ + _____

_____ = _____

Kay has _____ tamarind balls altogether.

b Jacques had 5 fudge sticks. His friend gave him 8 more.
How many does he have altogether?

_____ = the total number of fudge sticks

_____ = _____ + _____

_____ = _____

Jacques has _____ fudge sticks altogether.

Reasoning activity

Work in pairs and write word problems for each of these.

$x = 9 + 4$ $x = 12 + 7$

More problem solving

Write the number sentence for each problem and solve it.
The first one has been done for you.

1 Roy has 22 pens.
Jane has 17 pens.
They have 39 altogether.

_22_ + _17_ = _39_

2 Tom has 54 buttons.
He gives Pam 13 buttons.
Tom has ____ buttons left.

____ ____ = ____

3 Mary has $155.
She spends $14.
She has ____ left.

____ ____ = ____

4 Roy has 12 sweets.
Mary has 17 sweets.
Together they have
____ sweets.

____ ____ = ____

5 Tim has 10 pens.
Sandra has none.
They have ____
pens altogether.

____ ____ = ____

6 John collects 16 shells.
Sandra collects 13 shells.
They collected ____ shells
altogether.

____ ____ = ____

7 Jane has 25 mangoes.
She gives 5 to Tom.
Jane is left with ____
mangoes.

____ ____ = ____

8 Jane has 58 marbles.
She loses 4.
How many does she have
left? ____

____ ____ = ____

Try this

Act out each number story **with a partner** to help you
decide whether to add or subtract.

11 Shapes

Plane shapes

1 Look at these shapes. Answer the questions.

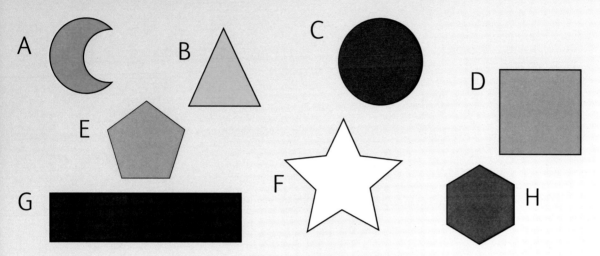

a Which shapes have straight sides? _____

b Which shapes have curved sides? _____

c Which shape has just 3 straight sides? _____

d How many straight sides does shape C have? _____

2 a Draw a shape with 4 straight sides.

b Draw a shape with 5 straight sides.

Try this

Draw a shape with 2 straight sides and 2 curved sides.
Draw a shape with straight sides, all the same length.

Reasoning activity

Draw five shapes, each with 4 straight sides.
Can you make each shape look different?

Solid shapes

Explain

Solid shapes are used for everyday items.
Look at these shapes.

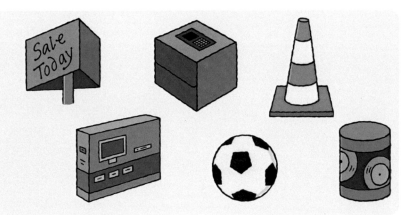

1 Write the name for each shape.

a

b

c

_____

_____

_____

d

e

f

_____

_____

_____

Reasoning activity

These boxes have been opened out. Colour the ones that have lids.

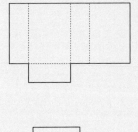
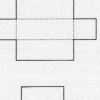
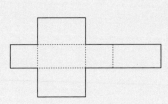

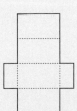
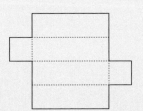

Sorting solid shapes

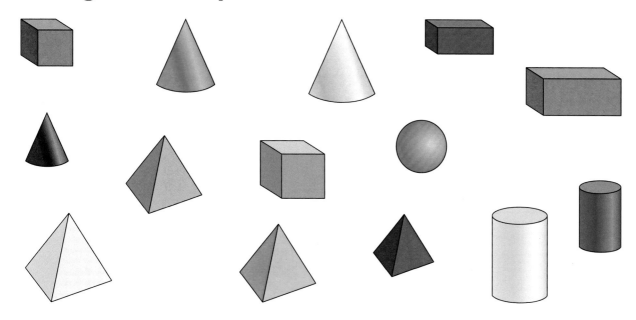

1 Sort some solid shapes in this sorting diagram.

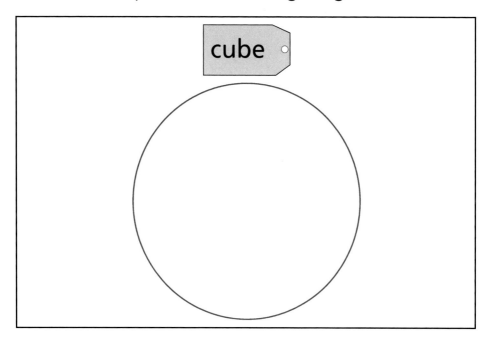

cube

2 Change the label in the sorting diagram. Choose one of these and then sort your shapes.

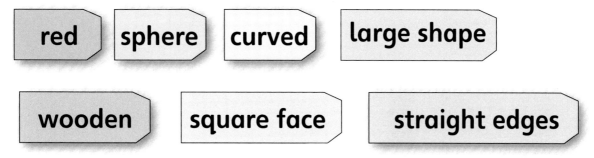

red sphere curved large shape

wooden square face straight edges

12 Algebra

Giving the missing number

Explain

4 + _____ = 10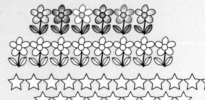

What is the missing number?
Use subtraction to help you find the missing number.
10 − 4 = 6   4 + 6 = 10

1 Use the sets to help you add.

a 6 + _____ = 14

b 12 + _____ = 21

c 8 + _____ = 20

Reasoning activity

Use the sets to make up your own calculations.

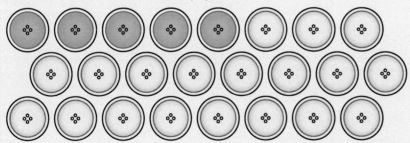

5 + _____ = 24

_____ + _____ = 24

24 − 5 = _____

24 − _____ = 5

What do you notice about the numbers 24, 5 and 19 in these additions and subtractions?
Write your own addition and then complete the family of addition and subtraction facts to match.

How many more? Countable things

Explain

$9 - 5 = n$

9 is 4 more than 5.

$9 - 5 = 4$

$n = 4$

$12 - 7 = n$

12 is 5 more than 7.

$12 - 7 = 5$

$n = 5$

Use lines of counters to help you solve these.

1 $13 - 5 = n$

   13 is _____ more than 5

   $13 - 5 =$ _____

   $n =$ _____

2 $23 - 6 = n$

   23 is _____ more than 6

   $23 - 6 =$ _____

   $n =$ _____

3 $27 - 8 = n$

   27 is _____ more than 8

   $n =$ _____

4 $19 - 7 = n$

   19 is _____ more than 7

   $n =$ _____

5 $18 - 9 = n$

   18 is _____ more than 9

   $n =$ _____

6 $25 - 6 = n$

   25 is _____ more than 6

   $n =$ _____

7 Maria, Lisa and Carole picked oranges.
Look at the picture and complete the
sentences.

   a Maria picked _____ more than Carole.

   b Lisa picked _____ more than Maria.

   c Lisa picked _____ more than Carole.

Maria   Lisa   Carole

Try this

How many more oranges did Marie and Carole
pick altogether than Lisa picked?

Using symbols to solve problems

Explain

Mike has 3 guineps. Jason gives him some more. Now he has 7.
How many guineps did Jason give Mike?

n = the number of guineps Jason gave Mike.

3 + *n* = 7

7 − 3 = 4

n = 4

This bar model shows 3 + *n* = 7

It also shows 7 − 3 = *n*

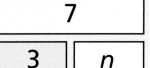

7	
3	*n*

1 Write the number sentence using *n*. Then work out the value of *n*.

a Mrs Habib sold 35 melons in one day. She sold 12 in the morning and the rest in the afternoon.

How many did she sell in the afternoon?

_____ + *n* = _____   *n* = _____

She sold _____ melons in the afternoon.

b Jenny has 32 marbles in her collection. Her brother gives her some more marbles. Now she has 48 altogether.

How many marbles did Jenny's brother give her?

_____ + *n* = _____   *n* = _____

Jenny's brother gave her _____ marbles.

c A vendor roasts 25 yams. She sells 1 3 yams. How many roasted yams does she have left?

_____ + *n* = _____   *n* = _____

She has _____ roasted yams left.

Reasoning activity

Write three different word problems that could be solved using this bar model.

45	
n	21

Assess and review

I can add and subtract tens, sort solid shapes and work out missing numbers in problems.

1 Complete the number sentences.

30 + 40 = _____   _____ + 70 = 90   50 + _____ = 80

60 − 20 = _____   _____ − 10 = 30   90 − _____ = 50

2 Sort these shapes. Draw lines to the correct names.

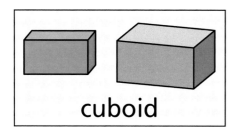

cuboid

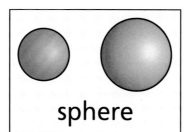

sphere

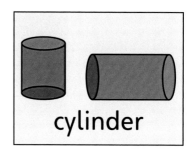

cylinder

3 Solve these problems. Work out the value of *n*.

a James has 12 marbles.
He gives some of them to a friend and has 7 left.

How many did he give to his friend?

$12 - n = 7$ $n =$ _____

b Lisa has some bananas in her bag.
She takes another bunch of 8 bananas so she has 20 altogether.

How many did she have in her bag to begin with?

$n + 8 = 20$ $n =$ _____

4 Write the missing numbers in the bricks.

37	
17	20

30	18

	29
	9

Extended Project 1

Sam's snack van

Sam has a snack van and his most popular food is his famous Big Burger. You can have a Big Burger with tomato or cheese if you want, or with both together.

- How many different sorts of burger could you buy? Give them special names. Colour the correct number to show the burgers and write their names.

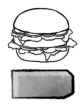   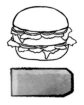

- What if he starts selling onions for his burger? How many different sorts of burger could you now buy?

- He then includes pickles to choose for your burger. How many different sorts of burger could you now buy?

These are the prices for his Big Burger.

- How many different ways could you spend $50 on extras?

- How many different ways could you spend $100 on extras?

Big Burger	$400
Extras:	
Cheese	$50
Tomatoes	$40
Onions	$30
Pickles	$20
Hot sauce	$10

Next step

Make up your own menu for a Big Burger. Include prices and different extras to have on the burger. Can you make the total price for a burger and three toppings exactly $500?

13 Adding and subtracting larger numbers

Number lines to model addition

+ is the sign for addition.

These are words that tell you to add.

When we add we make the number larger.
For example:

8 + 2 + 6

You can use a number line to help you to add.

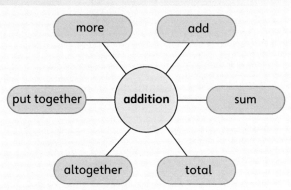

| 0 | 1 | 2 | 3 | 4 | 5 | 6 | 7 | 8 | 9 | 10 | 11 | 12 | 13 | 14 | 15 | 16 |

8 + 2 + 6 = 16

1 Add the numbers in the balloons. Write the answer.
Use the number line to help you.

a  4 + 3 + 2 = _____

b 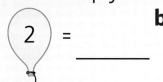 2 + 1 + 6 = _____

c  1 + 4 + 8 = _____

d 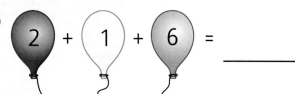 4 + 5 + 8 = _____

e  5 + 6 + 9 = _____

f 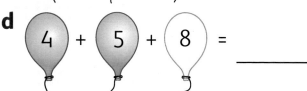 3 + 3 + 3 = _____

Reasoning activity

Add each number 1–5 to itself 3 times.

1+1+1 =   2 + 2 + 2 =   3 + 3 + 3 =   4 + 4 + 4 =   5 + 5 + 5 =

What do you notice about the answers? Can you give a rule for adding like this with larger numbers?

Adding with number lines

1 Draw number lines to help you to add.

  a Find the sum of 9 ripe bananas and 8 green bananas.

    _____ + _____ = _____

  b Harry ate 9 candies on Monday and 10 on Thursday.
     How many candies did Harry eat altogether?

    _____ + _____ = _____

  c Mr Brown has 4 horses, 5 donkeys, 3 hens and 6 cows.
     How many animals does he have altogether?

    _____ + _____ + _____ + _____ = _____

2 Add up all the numbers on each T-shirt.

  a

> **Remember**
>
> When adding on a number line, start with the largest number.

_____ + _____ + _____ + _____ + _____ + _____ = _____

  b

_____ + _____ + _____ + _____ + _____ + _____ = _____

Adding and subtracting

1 Subtract in columns.

a 38 – 17 = _____

Tens	Ones
3	8
– 1	7
___	___

b 42 – 12 = _____

Tens	Ones
4	2
– 1	2
___	___

c 55 – 5 = _____

Tens	Ones
5	5
–	5
___	___

d 65 – 4 = _____

Tens	Ones
6	5
–	4
___	___

2 Now try adding three numbers in columns.

a 10 + 11 + 12 = _____

Tens	Ones
1	0
1	1
+ 1	2
___	___

b 42 + 13 + 11 = _____

Tens	Ones
4	2
1	3
+ 1	1
___	___

c 4 + 14 + 11 = _____

Tens	Ones
	4
1	4
+ 1	1
___	___

d 3 + 24 + 2 = _____

Tens	Ones
	3
2	4
+	2
___	___

Remember

When calculating using columns, add or subtract the ones and then the tens.

How many more?

June makes bracelets at the craft market.
A small bracelet uses 63 beads.
A large bracelet uses 78 beads.

1 How many more beads does June
need to make a small bracelet?

a  63 – 12 = 51

She needs 51 more beads.

Tens	Ones
6	3
– 1	2
5	1

b 63 – _____ = _____

She needs _____ .

Tens	Ones
6	3
–	

c  63 – _____ = _____

She needs _____ .

Tens	Ones
6	3
–	

2 How many beads must June add to
these to make a large bracelet?

a  78 – _____ = _____

She needs _____ .

Tens	Ones
7	8
–	

b 78 – _____ = _____

She needs _____ .

Tens	Ones
7	8
–	

Reasoning activity

June has 18 spare beads. She decides to break
up a small bracelet and use these beads with the
spares to make a large bracelet.

Has she got enough beads to do this?

Basic operations

1 Add.

a 23	**b** 61	**c** 14	**d** 27	**e** 35
+ 35	+ 25	+ 82	+ 32	+ 53

f 20	**g** 15	**h** 16	**i** 23	**j** 13
24	21	21	15	22
+ 22	+ 32	+ 52	+ 21	+ 34

2 Subtract.

25	63	84	19	27	69
− 21	− 42	− 51	− 12	− 11	− 25

Try this

Look at the graph below. How many minutes did Gavin spend at the park altogether? _____

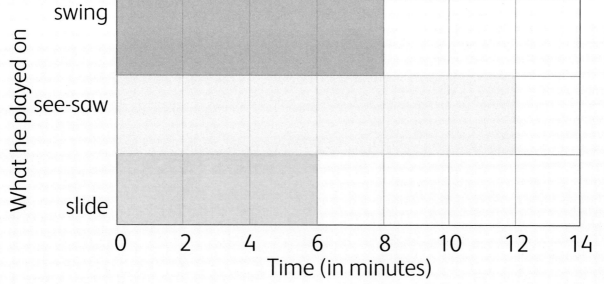

Gavin's time at the park

Adding 3-digit numbers

Explain

You can add **in columns**.

251 + 16 = _____

H	T	O
2	5	1
+	1	6
2	6	7

403 + 125 = _____

H	T	O
4	0	3
+ 1	2	5
5	2	8

You can also add using **expanded notation**.
Group the hundreds, tens and ones so they are easy to add.

251 + 16

= 200 + 50 + 1 + 10 + 6

= 200 + 50 + 10 + 1 + 6

= 200 + 60 + 7

= 267

403 + 125

= 400 + 3 + 100 + 20 + 5

= 400 + 100 + 20 + 3 + 5

= 500 + 20 + 8

= 528

1 Add in columns.

   a 434 + 245 = _____   **b** 682 + 203 = _____

2 Add using expanded notation.

   a 250 + 108 = _____   **b** 713 + 142 = _____

   c 520 + 421 = _____   **d** 201 + 102 = _____

Reasoning activity

Use the digits 2, 3 and 4 to make
different 3-digit numbers, such as 324.
Add pairs of your numbers together.
What is the largest total you can make?
Which is the smallest total you can make?

3	2	4

Subtracting 3-digit numbers

Explain

In columns

378 – 125 = _____

H	T	O
3	7	8
– 1	2	5
2	5	3

Expanded notation

378 = 300 + 70 + 8
– 125 = 100 + 20 + 5
= 200 + 50 + 3
= 253

1 Subtract. Use expanded notation.

a 456 – 16 = _____

b 559 – 50 = _____

c 348 – 125 = _____

d 793 – 481 = _____

2 Subtract. Work in columns.

a 187 – 65 = _____

b 298 – 188 = _____

c 747 – 325 = _____

d 684 – 354 = _____

3 Complete these, writing in the missing digits.

a 3 ☐ 4 – 124 = ☐ 60

b 63 ☐ – 5 ☐ 3 = 132

c ☐ 63 – 1 ☐ 2 = 72 ☐

d 5 ☐ 9 – 35 ☐ = ☐ 35

Reasoning activity

Compare the two methods. What is the same and what is different?

Working with 3-digit numbers

1 Add. Use the method that you find easiest.

a 732 + 100 = _____

b 486 + 300 = _____

c 134 + 500 = _____

d 112 + 107 = _____

e 234 + 122 = _____

f 563 + 130 = _____

2 Subtract. Use the method you find easiest.

a 529 – 19 = _____

b 435 – 4 = _____

c 783 – 120 = _____

d 655 – 14 = _____

e 299 – 188 = _____

f 385 – 275 = _____

Reasoning activity

Work in groups and take turns to each explain the method you used for one of the additions in question 1. Did anyone use a different method for the same addition?

Repeat, explaining the methods used for each subtraction in question 2.

Using subtraction to compare sets

What is the **difference** between these two sets?

H	T	O
1	9	2
–	7	0
1	2	2

Subtract the smaller number from the bigger number to compare.

There are 122 more apples than oranges.

The difference is 122.

192	
70	?

1 Use subtraction to find the difference between the sets.

a

There are _____ more pineapples than apples.

H	T	O
2	7	6
– 1	5	3

b

There are _____ more mangoes than pears.

H	T	O
3	6	4
– 2	0	3

Try this

a There are 548 pears and 146 apples. How many more pears than apples?

_____ – _____ = _____

b There are 898 plums and 590 bananas. What is the difference?

_____ – _____ = _____

Remember

Finding the difference means subtracting. Identify the smaller number and subtract it from the larger number. A bar model can help you work out what you are trying to find.

Partitioning and renaming

What do you notice about these additions?

$37 + 6 \rightarrow 30 + 7 + 6 \rightarrow 30 + 13 \rightarrow 30 + 10 + 3 = 43$

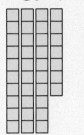  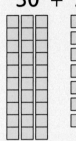  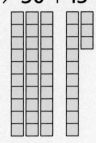 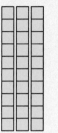 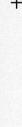

$46 + 28$

$\begin{array}{r} 40 + 6 \\ + \ 20 + 8 \\ \hline 60 + 14 \end{array}$ $\quad 60 + 10 + 4 = 74$

1 Use rods and cubes to add these pairs of numbers.

a $48 + 7 =$ ___   **b** $39 + 7 =$ ___   **c** $44 + 9 =$ ___

2 Complete these additions.

a
$\begin{array}{r} 30 + 8 \\ + \ 10 + 4 \\ \hline \_\_ + \_\_ \\ \hline \end{array}$

b
$\begin{array}{r} 20 + 5 \\ + \ 30 + 6 \\ \hline \_\_ + \_\_ \\ \hline \end{array}$

c
$\begin{array}{r} 30 + 4 \\ + \ 10 + 9 \\ \hline \_\_ + \_\_ \\ \hline \end{array}$

d
$\begin{array}{r} 40 + 4 \\ + \ 20 + 7 \\ \hline \_\_ + \_\_ \\ \hline \end{array}$

e
$\begin{array}{r} 40 + 6 \\ + \ 30 + 6 \\ \hline \_\_ + \_\_ \\ \hline \end{array}$

f
$\begin{array}{r} 50 + 7 \\ + \ 30 + 8 \\ \hline \_\_ + \_\_ \\ \hline \end{array}$

Try this

Could you do this for this 3-digit addition?

$\begin{array}{r} 100 + 20 \ + \ 5 \\ + \ 200 + 30 \ + \ 8 \\ \hline \_\_ + \_\_ + \_\_ \\ \hline \end{array}$

Remember

Check your answers with the numbers you added. Does it all look correct?

Addition with renaming

Explain

25 + 18 = _____

Tens	Ones
2^1	5
+ 1	8
4	3

First add the ones.
5 + 8 = 13
13 = 1 ten 3 ones
Write 3 in the ones column.
Carry 1 to the tens column.
Now add the tens.
1 ten + 2 tens + 1 ten = 4 tens.
Write the 4 in the tens column.
25 + 18 = 43

1 Add in columns.

a 37 + 24 = _____

Tens	Ones
3	7
+ 2	4
—	—

b 53 + 19 = _____

Tens	Ones
5	3
+ 1	9
—	—

c 34 + 36 = _____

Tens	Ones
—	—

d 72 + 18 = _____

Tens	Ones
—	—

e 45 + 45 = _____

Tens	Ones
—	—

f 39 + 23 = _____

Tens	Ones
—	—

Reasoning activity

Can you add 13 and 25 in your head? Explain your method.

Subtraction with renaming

Explain

Look at this method of subtraction.

$$\begin{array}{r} {}^{4}\cancel{5}{}^{1}3 \\ -\ 38 \\ \hline 15 \end{array}$$

$$\begin{array}{r} 40 + 13 \\ -\ 30 + 8 \\ \hline -\ 10 + 5 \end{array}$$

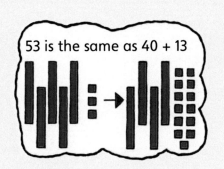

53 is the same as 40 + 13

One ten is exchanged and 53 is renamed as 40 and 13.

1
$$\begin{array}{r} 42 \\ -\ 16 \\ \hline \\ \hline \end{array}$$

2
$$\begin{array}{r} 35 \\ -\ 17 \\ \hline \\ \hline \end{array}$$

3
$$\begin{array}{r} 91 \\ -\ 43 \\ \hline \\ \hline \end{array}$$

4
$$\begin{array}{r} 75 \\ -\ 69 \\ \hline \\ \hline \end{array}$$

5
$$\begin{array}{r} 67 \\ -\ 38 \\ \hline \\ \hline \end{array}$$

6
$$\begin{array}{r} 70 \\ -\ 25 \\ \hline \\ \hline \end{array}$$

Try this

a Take 57 from 83.

b From 94 take 46.

c Subtract 29 from 51.

d Raymond had 62 marbles.

He gave 18 to Paul.

How many marbles does Raymond have now?

Remember

You can use rods and cubes to help you exchange and rename. Make your crossing out and renaming very clear on your work.

Calendar of events

Try this

Use a calendar to help you complete the sentences.

a Today is _____ the _____ of _____ .
                     (day)   (date)   (month and year)

b Last month was _____ .

c Next month will be _____ .

d Christmas is _____ months from now.

Explain

1 January	New Year's Day
6 February	Bob Marley's birthday
1 May	National Labour Day
23 May	Labour Day
1 August	Emancipation Day
6 August	Independence Day
25 December	Christmas Day

Hurricane season starts in June and ends in November.
Summer holidays start in July and end in September.

1 a The first day of the year is _____ .

  b Bob Marley's birthday is _____ months before Independence Day.

  c Emancipation Day is _____ days after National Labour Day.

  d Christmas Day is _____ months after New Year's Day.

  e The hurricane season is _____ months long.

  f Summer holidays are _____ months long.

Reasoning activity

Work in pairs with a calendar. Write how many days there are in each month. Use a calculator to add them up. What is the total for the year?

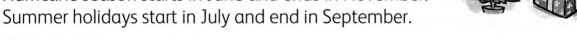

Understanding calendars

1 Put the days in the right order, starting with Sunday.

Wednesday, Friday, Tuesday, Sunday, Monday, Saturday, Thursday.

_____ _____

_____ _____

_____ _____

_____

2 Number the months from 1st to 12th.

March _____   December _____

July _____   November _____

April _____   January _____

August _____   October _____

May _____   February _____

June _____   September _____

Try this

Amy's birthday is on 5th January. Jamie's birthday is on 18th January. Carla's birthday is on 22nd January. Eli's birthday is on 31 January.

Write their names on the correct days in the calendar.

Find out if anyone in your class has a birthday in January.

Fill in their names on the correct day.

JANUARY

		1	2	3	4	5
6	7	8	9	10	11	12
13	14	15	16	17	18	19
20	21	22	23	24	25	26
27	28	29	30	31		

Reasoning activity

Work in pairs. How long until your next birthday? Decide how you will write each answer. Will it be in days, weeks or months? Who will have their birthday first?

Telling the time

The minute hand is long.
The hour hand is short.
The minute hand is pointing to 12.
The hour hand is pointing to 8.
It is 8 o'clock.

1 Write the time shown on each clock.

_____ o'clock   _____ o'clock   _____ o'clock   _____ o'clock

2 Write the missing numbers on the clocks.

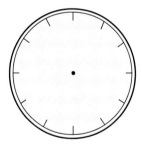 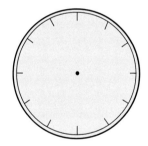 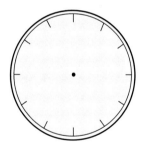

7 o'clock   3 o'clock   11 o'clock

3 Draw hands to show the times.

Reasoning activity

Work in groups and describe the difference between daytime and nighttime?
How many hours of daytime do we have each day?

Remember

It is the short hand that shows you which hour it is. If the hour hand is
between two numbers it shows it is past an hour. For example, if the hand is
between 3 and 4 the time is 'past 3 o'clock'.

Half hours

These clocks show these times:

- half past two
- half past eleven
- half past eight

Can you work out which clock shows which time?

There are 60 minutes in an hour. The long minute hand is half way round, so 30 minutes past the hour. This shows it is half past the hour.

1 Write the time shown on each clock.

half past three _____ _____ _____

2 Circle yes or no.

 Yes   No

half past twelve

 Yes   No

half past one

 Yes   No

half past ten

3 Draw the missing hands to show the time.

half past three   half past seven   half past ten

Remember

At half past the hour, the short hand does not point directly towards the number of the hour. At half past, it will be halfway between the hour mark and the next hour mark.

Try this

How do we show time on a digital clock?

Matching times

These two clocks show the same time.

Analogue clock

$8:30$

Digital clock

What is the same and what is different about the two clocks?

1 Find matching times. Colour the matching clocks the same colour.

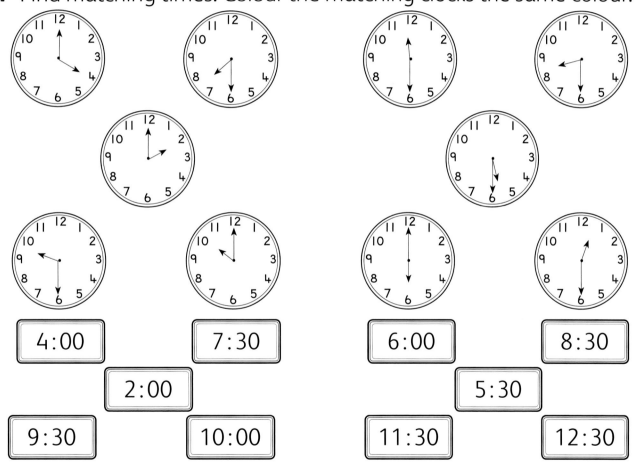

| 4:00 | 7:30 | 6:00 | 8:30 |

| 2:00 | | 5:30 | |

| 9:30 | 10:00 | 11:30 | 12:30 |

Reasoning activity

Work in pairs and start at 8.30. You always add 30 minutes and your partner always adds 1 hour. Take turns to say the new time until you reach 8.30. Repeat. Do you always end exactly on 8.30? Why or why not? Try with other times.

Time in hours

1 Read each pair of clocks. How many hours have passed?

a School started at _____ .
School finished at _____ .
How long was the school day?
____ hours

b The game started at _____ .
The game finished at _____ .
How long was the game?
____ hour

c Alan left home at _____ .
He got to school at _____ .
How long did he take?
____ hour

d Ray started painting at _____ .
He worked until _____ .
How long did he work?
____ hours

e Nicky started riding her bicycle
at _____ .
She finished at _____ .
How long did Nicky ride her
bicycle? ____ hours

Remember

To work out time differences, count on from the start time in hours
and then in half hours. For example, from 2.30 to 5.00 count on
2.30 → 3.30 → 4.30 → 5.00. So this is $2\frac{1}{2}$ hours.

Finishing times

What time did it finish? Fill in the table.

 The movie started at 6 o'clock. It took 2 hours. What time did it finish?

8 o'clock

 We went to the beach at 10 o'clock. We stayed for 3 hours. What time did we go home?

 The lesson started at 11 o'clock. It lasted 1 hour. What time did it finish?

 The party started at half past 4. We stayed for 2 hours. What time did it finish?

 We went to the park at 3 o'clock. We stayed for $1\frac{1}{2}$ hours. What time did we go home?

 The train left at 8 o'clock. The trip was 5 hours long. What time did it finish?

How long did it take?

1 George went to the Denbigh show. Read what he did.

from until

Went to see the horses

from until

Went to see the cows

from until

Went to see the birds

from until

Went on a donkey ride

2 How many minutes did it take?
Circle the correct answer.

   a Looking at the horses   10 15 30

   b Looking at the cows   15 20 25

   c Looking at the birds   10 15 30

   d Going on a donkey ride   10 30 20

Try this

How many minutes does it take to tie your shoelaces/do your homework/walk the dog? How many hours does it take to drive to the next parish?

Daily events

Explain

Times from midnight to 12 noon are called **a.m. times**.
Times after 12 noon to the next midnight are called **p.m. times**.

Circle a.m. or p.m. for each time.

a getting up 7:00 a.m. p.m.

b eating breakfast 7:30 a.m. p.m.

c school begins 8:00 a.m. p.m.

d eat lunch 12:30 a.m. p.m.

e school ends 2:00 a.m. p.m.

f eat dinner 5:00 a.m. p.m.

g do homework 6:30 a.m. p.m.

h brush teeth before bed 7:30 a.m. p.m.

Reasoning activity

In groups talk about these statements.
Alba has a swimming lesson at 8 today.
Mr Green's flight is at 6.30 tomorrow.

Units of time

We measure time in :
- seconds • minutes
- hours • days
- weeks • months • years

60 seconds = 1 minute
60 minutes = 1 hour
24 hours = 1 day
7 days = 1 week
12 months = 1 year

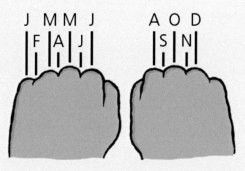

The knuckle months all have 31 days. The months between the knuckle bones have 30 days except February, which has 28 days.

1 Use units of times to complete each sentence.

   a She ate a patty within 15 _____ .

   b 120 _____ equals 2 minutes.

   c My grandmother is 85 _____ old.

   d Usain Bolt ran the 100 m in less than 10 _____ .

2 Which unit of time would you use to measure these?

   a The time you take to brush your teeth. _____

   b The time a doctor would take to perform a heart surgery. _____

   c The time spent at home during the summer holidays. _____

   a Research and find out how many days are in 1 year. _____
   b What is a decade?

_____

_____

Assess and review

I can add and subtract 2-digit numbers and some 3-digit numbers, talk about units of time, read the time to the half hour and say how long something took to happen.

1 Work out these. Show the method you use.

152 + 36 = _____   305 + 193 = _____

283 – 51 = _____   415 – 102 = _____

2 Work out these.

```
    66          58          87          71
  + 27        + 35        – 59        – 48
  ────        ────        ────        ────

  ────        ────        ────        ────
```

3 Complete these.

_____ days = 2 weeks   _____ minutes = 2 hours

_____ months = 2 years

4 Write these times.

_____   _____   _____   _____

5 Draw the hands on these clocks to show the finish times.

   a A film started at 5 o'clock and lasted for $1\frac{1}{2}$ hours. What time did it finish?

   b A bus left the town at half past 11. It took $2\frac{1}{2}$ hours to reach the village. What time did it arrive at the village?

15 Using numbers

Odd and even

Explain

We can model numbers using rows of dots.
What numbers are these?
Divide each set of dots into pairs.
If there are no dots left over the number is **even**.
If there is one dot left over the number is **odd**.

a ●○○●●
   ●○○●○

b ●○○●○○●
   ●○○○●●○

c ●○●●○●○○
   ●○○○○●●○

Which of the numbers above are odd?
Which are even?

1 Circle pairs of dots.
   a Write the total number of dots.
   b Write odd or even next to each number.

__ _____   __ _____   __ _____   __ _____

__ _____   __ _____   __ _____   __ _____

2 Write odd or even next to each number.

   2 _____   8 _____   20 _____   23 _____

   3 _____   12 _____   17 _____   1 _____

Reasoning activity

Work in pairs and each draw a number line 1-20.
You start at 1 and your partner starts at 2. Both of you count on in twos, and circle the numbers you land on.
What do you notice?

Numbers that come next

1 Write the next three house numbers in each row.

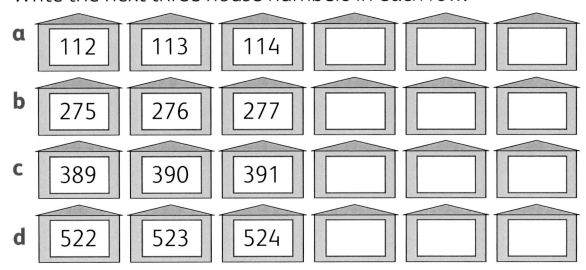

a 112 113 114 ☐ ☐ ☐

b 275 276 277 ☐ ☐ ☐

c 389 390 391 ☐ ☐ ☐

d 522 523 524 ☐ ☐ ☐

2 Write the next four numbers on each number line.

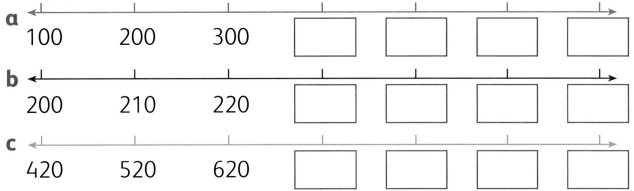

a 100   200   300   ☐ ☐ ☐ ☐

b 200   210   220   ☐ ☐ ☐ ☐

c 420   520   620   ☐ ☐ ☐ ☐

3 Continue each number pattern.

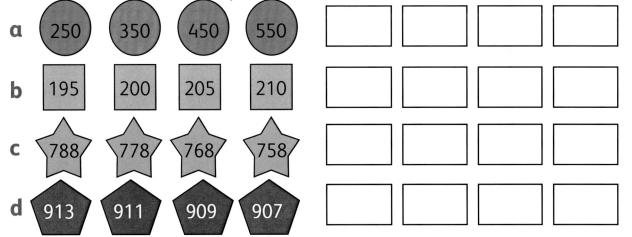

a 250 350 450 550   ☐ ☐ ☐ ☐

b 195 200 205 210   ☐ ☐ ☐ ☐

c 788 778 768 758   ☐ ☐ ☐ ☐

d 913 911 909 907   ☐ ☐ ☐ ☐

Remember

When you look at number patterns ask yourself these two questions.
Does the pattern count forwards (getting bigger) or backwards (getting
smaller)? By how much do the numbers get bigger or smaller each time?

Equal parts of a whole

Explain

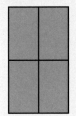 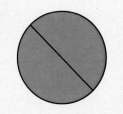

Some parts are **equal**.
This means the parts are the same size.

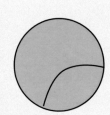

Some parts are **unequal**.
This means they are different sizes.

1 Write the number of parts for each shape below.
2 Circle whether the parts are equal or unequal.

a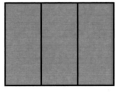

_____ parts

equal

unequal

b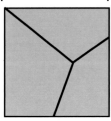

_____ parts

equal

unequal

c

_____ parts

equal

unequal

d

_____ parts

equal

unequal

e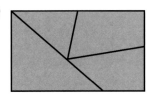

_____ parts

equal

unequal

f

_____ parts

equal

unequal

g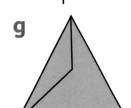

_____ parts

equal

unequal

h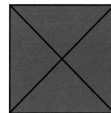

_____ parts

equal

unequal

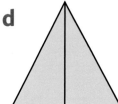

Reasoning activity

Two friends share a pizza. Jade will slice the pizza into 2 parts, but
her friend will take the first slice. How do you think Jade will slice the pizza?
In equal or unequal parts? Why?

Half of a shape

1 Colour half of each shape.

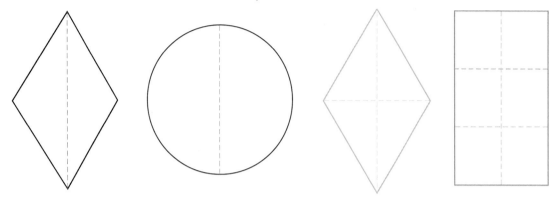

2 Which shapes are divided in half?
Tick those that show halves. Cross those that do not.

3 Draw one line to divide each shape into two halves.

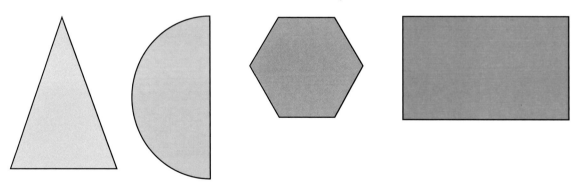

 **Remember**

A half is one out of two equal parts that make up the whole ($\frac{1}{2}$).
The parts must be equal, or they are not halves.

Half of an object

1 Circle the objects that are divided in half.

    a    **b** 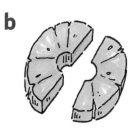   **c**    **d**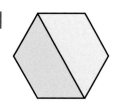

2 Colour $\frac{1}{2}$ of each object or set.

    a 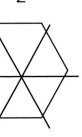   **b** 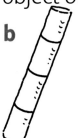   **c** 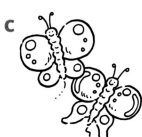   **d**

3 Circle half of the objects in each set.

    a    **b**

    c    **d**

Try this

How many children are there in half of your class?

Reasoning activity

Work in groups. When do we use halves in real life?

Half of a set

1 Circle half of each set.

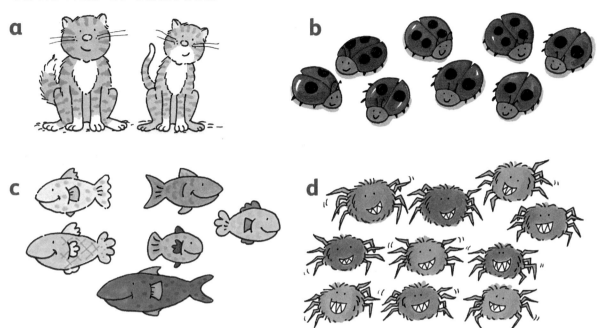

a

b

c

d

2 Cross out half the members of each set.

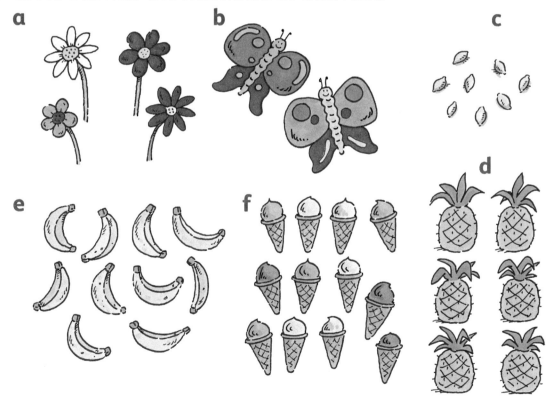

a

b

c

d

e

f

Half of a whole and a set

1 Nina cuts her fruit in half. Write $\frac{1}{2}$ next to Nina's fruit.

2 Colour $\frac{1}{2}$ of each set of flowers. Complete the sentences.

Half of 14 is ____ .

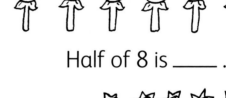

Half of 8 is ____ .

Half of 12 is ____ .

Half of 14 is ____ .

3 Colour $\frac{1}{2}$ of each shape.

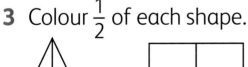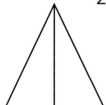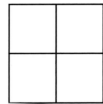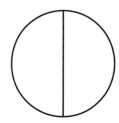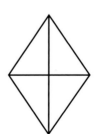

Reasoning activity

What do you notice about the number of parts you have shaded in question 3?
Work in groups and explain how 2 or 3 parts shaded can still be half.

Double and half

1 Colour half. Write the answers.

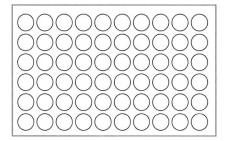 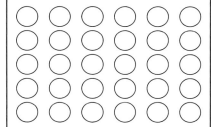 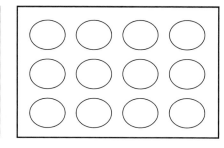

Half of 60 = _____   Half of 30 = _____   Half of 12 = _____

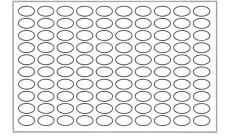 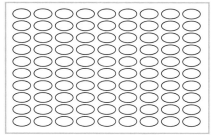 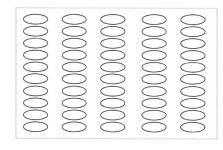

Half of 100 = _____   Half of 90 = _____   Half of 50 = _____

2 Draw dots to double each amount. Fill in the total.

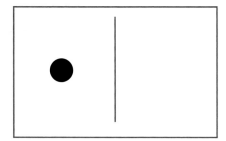 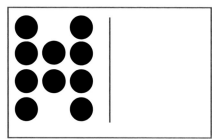 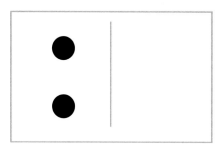

Double 1 = _____   Double 10 = _____   Double 2 = _____

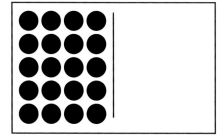 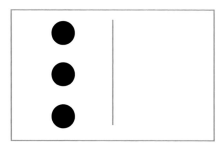 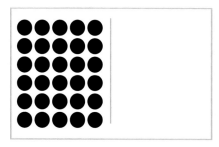

Double 20 = _____   Double 3 = _____   Double 30 = _____

Reasoning activity

What do you notice about the relationship between doubling and halving?

Quarter of a shape

1 Colour the shapes that are divided into quarters.

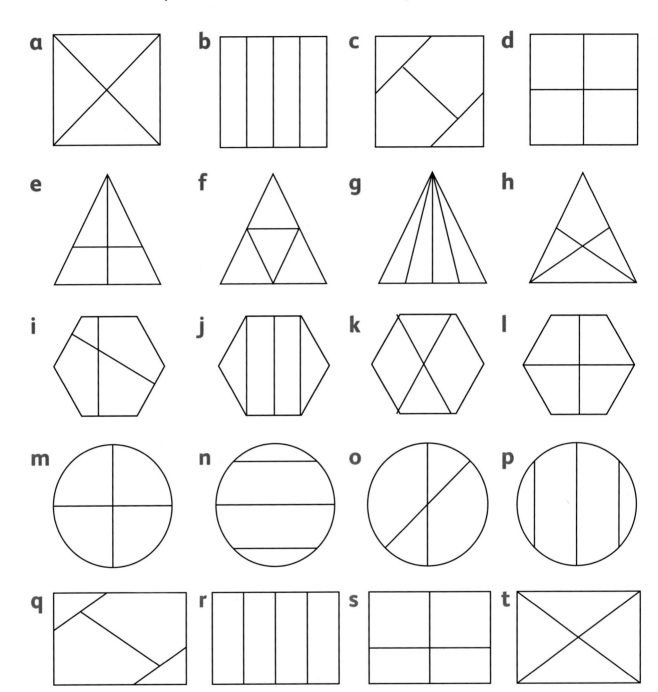

Remember

A shape, set or object is only divided into quarters when all the four parts are equal.

94

Quarter of a whole and a set

1 Gary cuts his fruit in quarters. Write $\frac{1}{4}$ next to Gary's fruit.

2 Colour $\frac{1}{4}$ of each set. Write the number.

A quarter of 4 is _____.   A quarter of 8 is _____.

A quarter of 16 is _____.   A quarter of 24 is _____.

3 Colour $\frac{1}{4}$ of each shape.

 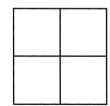   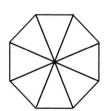

Try this

Take a sheet of paper. Fold it in half, then in half again.
Open the paper, how many parts are there?
Explain what happens when you halve a half.

95

16 Money

Jamaican notes and coins

1 Match each Jamaican coin or note to its value.
Write the value of each coin or note.

a
b
c

_____   _____   _____

d
e

_____   _____

f
g
h

_____   _____

five hundred dollars   one dollar   a thousand dollars

five dollars   a hundred dollars   ten dollars

twenty dollars   fifty dollars

Try this

Count in hundreds. How many $100 notes
do you need to make the the same value as one
$1000 note?

More about coins

Explain

We can make up money amounts using different coins and notes.
Here are some different ways to make up **20** dollars:

 =  =

1 Write the total value of each set.
Then draw a different set of coins to make up the same value.
The first one has been done for you.

$5 + $5 + $5 = $15

_____

_____

_____

Reasoning activity

Work in pairs with $1 and $5 coins. How many different ways can you make $20?

Make up totals

1 Write the total value of each set.
Then work out how many 10c coins make up the same value.

	Total value	How many 10c
25c 25c 25c 25c 25c 25c		
25c 10c 25c 10c 25c 25c		
10c 10c 25c 10c 25c		

 **Try this**

Write the total value of each set. Then work out how many
$10 coins you would need to make up the same value.

	Total value	How many $10
$5 $5 $5 $5		
$5 $5 $5 $5 $10 $10		
$20 $20 $10 $10		

Adding prices

Write the total, and the change.

Price	Money I have	Change
$20	$1 $1 $1 $1 $1 $5 $10 _____	_____ dollars
$40	$1 $1 $1 $5 $5 $5 $5 $10 $10 _____	_____ dollars
$76	$20 $20 $20 $20 _____	_____ dollars
$99	$100 _____	_____ dollars
$85	$100 _____	_____ dollars
$96	$100 _____	_____ dollars
$49	$20 $20 $10 _____	_____ dollars

 **Try this**

Role play shopping with friends where you 'buy' items of given prices and work out the total and the change in dollars.

Shopping

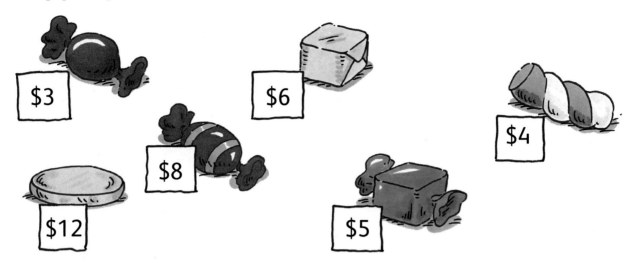

1 Complete these.

    a 🍬 + 🍪 cost $_____ .

    b 🍬 🍬 + 🍫 cost $_____ .

    c 🍬 🍬 🍬 cost $_____ .

    d 🍬 and 📦 cost $_____ .

2 Complete these.

    a Buy 🍬 🍬 with **$20**.   Get $_____ change.

    b Buy 🍬 🍬 🍬 with **$20**. Get $_____ change.

    c Buy 📦 📦 with **$15**.   Get $_____ change.

3 Draw the sweets you can buy with:

    a **$5** or less   **b** **$16**

    c **$20**   **d** **$10**

Try this

Work in pairs.
How many of each sweet can you buy for $25?
What change will you get?

Capacity of containers

Explain

Capacity is the amount that a container can hold.

Sam   Lulu   Andrew   Shaun   Priya   Rufus

1 Each container is filled with liquid.
  a Who gets the most? _____
  b Who gets the least? _____
  c Write the names in order from who gets most to who gets least.

  _____   _____   _____   _____   _____   _____

Reasoning activity

Work in groups and decide if this statement is true.
Tall containers always hold more water than short containers.

Try this

Use any two containers, such as a bottle, jug or cup.
How could you prove that one container holds more water than the other? Find two different ways to show this.

Comparing capacity

You need some different containers.
Draw them or write their names in the left hand column.
a Guess how many cups of water each container can hold.
b Measure how much each container can hold.

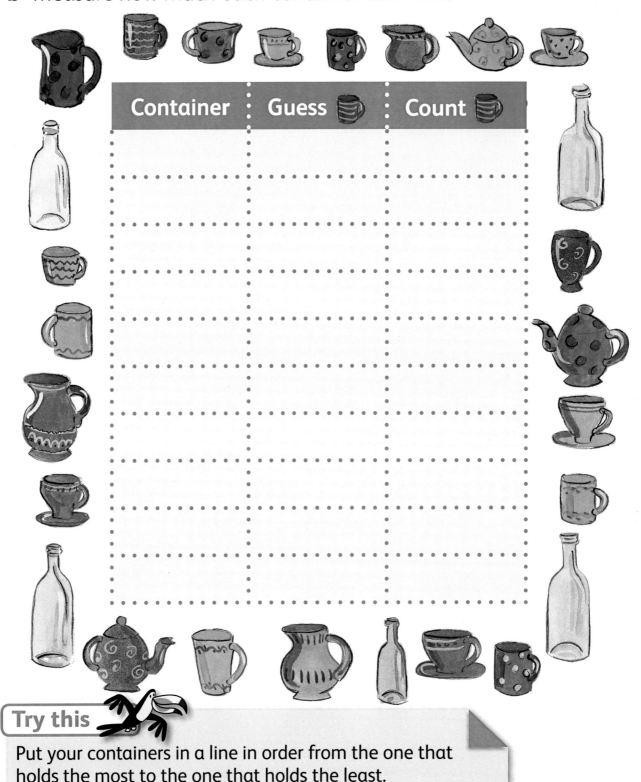

Container	Guess	Count

Try this

Put your containers in a line in order from the one that holds the most to the one that holds the least.

Litres and half litres

We measure capacity in **litres** (l).

 = 1 cup    = 1 litre    = $\frac{1}{2}$ litre

 =

4 cups makes 1 litre   2 cups makes $\frac{1}{2}$ litre

1 How many cups?

a  _____

b _____

c  _____

d  _____

2 How many litres?

a _____

c _____

d  _____

b  _____

Test the relationship between cups, litres and half litres. Try filling a litre bottle with four cups, or a half-litre bottle with two cups of water.

Comparing litre amounts

1 Fill in <, > or = to make these true.

a

b

c

d

e

f

g

Remember

Do you remember the < and > symbols? The open
side of the symbol opens towards the larger value.

Assess and review

I can work out halves and quarters of a shape or objects, use coins and notes for shopping and estimate and measure the capacity of containers using litres.

1 Colour $\frac{1}{2}$ of each shape.

  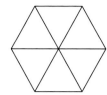

2 Colour $\frac{1}{4}$ of each shape.

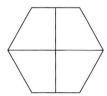

3 Colour the stars to show each fraction. Write the answers.

$\frac{1}{2}$ of 12 = ___

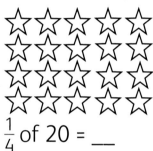

$\frac{1}{4}$ of 20 = ___

4 Write the total and the change.

Price	Money I have	Change	
$62	$10 $10 $10 $20 $20 _____	_____ dollars	
$86	$50 $50 $50 $50 _____	_____ dollars	

5 Use different measuring jugs.

Measure and find a container that holds about 1 litre and another that holds about $\frac{1}{2}$ litre. Draw them here.

Adding and multiplying

Explain

How many sets of 3?
2 sets of 3
Two 3s are 6
$2 \times 3 = 6$
× means **times** or **multiply**.

3 + 3 = 6

1 Complete the number sentences.

a

_____ sets of 2

2 + 2 + 2 + 2 = _____ $4 \times 2 =$ _____

b

_____ sets of 2

2 + 2 = _____ $2 \times 2 =$ _____

c

_____ sets of 3

3 + 3 + 3 = _____ $3 \times 3 =$ _____

d

_____ sets of 4

4 + 4 + 4 + 4 + 4 = _____ $5 \times 4 =$ _____

Try this

Use 12 counters.
Put them in groups to show repeated addition, such as 3 + 3 + 3 + 3.
Write this as a multiplication.
Repeat this for other groups.

Multiplying in rows and columns

Explain

4 per row.
3 per column.
4 × 3 = 12
There are 12 presents altogether.

These are arranged in an **array**.
How many presents are there?

1 How many are there altogether? Multiply using rows and columns.

a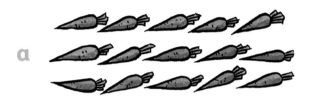

_____ per row

_____ per column

__ × __ = __ and __ × __ = __

_____ altogether.

b

_____ per row

_____ per column

__ × __ = __ and __ × __ = __

_____ altogether.

c

_____ per row

_____ per column

__ × __ = __ and __ × __ = __

_____ altogether.

d

_____ per row

_____ per column

__ × __ = __ and __ × __ = __

_____ altogether.

Reasoning activity

A gardener has 24 seeds to plant in rows. Each row must have the same number of seeds.

How many different ways can the seeds be planted?

Record your results as: ___ x ___ rows = 24

Arrays of multiplication facts

We can multiply in different ways.

In an array the shapes are arranged in rows and columns.

Arrays can help us to multiply.

There are 2 rows of 3 dots.

3 + 3 = 6	2 sets of 3 = 6	2 × 3 = 6

There are 3 columns of 2 dots.

2 + 2 + 2 = 6	3 sets of 2 = 6	3 × 2 = 6

1 Use the arrays to help you multiply.

a

 3 × 5 = _____

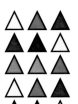 5 × 3 = _____

b

 4 × 2 = _____

 2 × 4 = _____

c

 3 × 6 = _____

 6 × 3 = _____

d

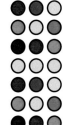 7 × 3 = _____

 3 × 7 = _____

Reasoning activity

Work in groups and think where you find rows and columns of objects in real life.

How would you write rows and columns of eggs in boxes?

Do you think it is 2 x 3 or 3 x 2?

More arrays

1 Write multiplication sentences for these.

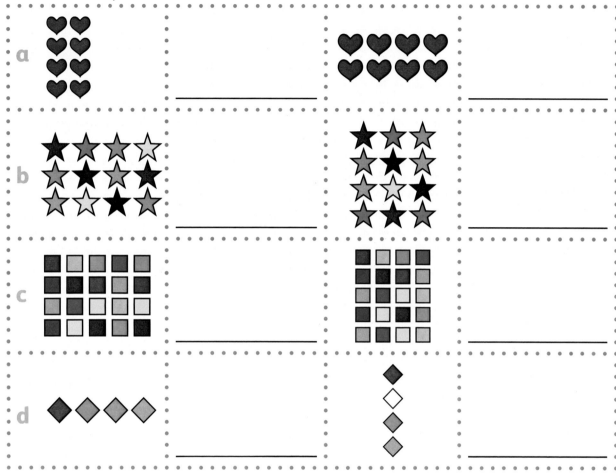

2 Use beans or counters to show these.

    a 4 rows of 7   b 8 rows of 4   c 5 rows of 5

    d 4 rows of 8   e 7 rows of 3   f 9 rows of 4

3 Use arrays of objects to help you solve these.
   Draw the rows and write the multiplication sentence.

    a There are 7 rows of coconut trees, with 6 trees in each row.

       ___ × ___ = ___

    b Sanya puts eggs in rows of 6 in a tray. She fills the tray with
       30 eggs. How many columns does she make? ___ × ___ = ___

Reasoning activity

Work with the whole class. Work out multiplication sentences for these:
Hold hands with a partner and line up in twos. Now drop hands and make two lines.
Try this with different numbers of classmates.

Multiplication sentences

Jamie has 3 baskets with 4 flowers in each basket.
How many flowers are there altogether?

4 + 4 + 4 = _____

3 × 4 = _____

How many altogether?

1 a

2 × 6 = _____

b

4 × 5 = _____

c Ally has 3 dogs. She gave each dog 8 bones.
How many bones have the dogs received?

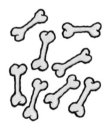  

_____

2 Draw pictures to show these problems and solve them.

a Tia bought 3 packs of crayons. Each pack has 10 crayons.
How many crayons are there in total?

b There are 5 boxes with 12 oranges in each box.
How many oranges are there in total?

Multiplication on a number line

Explain

You can count in different steps on a number line.

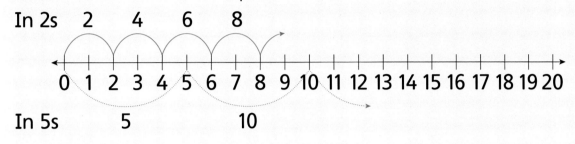

In 2s   2   4   6   8

0 1 2 3 4 5 6 7 8 9 10 11 12 13 14 15 16 17 18 19 20

In 5s   5   10

What are the next steps?

1   Count in steps on these number lines.

    a   Count in 2s.

0 1 2 3 4 5 6 7 8 9 10 11 12 13 14 15 16 17 18 19 20

    b   Count in 3s.

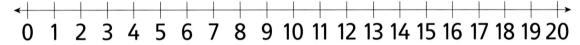

0 1 2 3 4 5 6 7 8 9 10 11 12 13 14 15 16 17 18 19 20

    c   Count in 4s.

0 1 2 3 4 5 6 7 8 9 10 11 12 13 14 15 16 17 18 19 20

    d   Count in 5s.

0 1 2 3 4 5 6 7 8 9 10 11 12 13 14 15 16 17 18 19 20

2   Complete these.

    a   Count in 2s for 5 steps is $5 \times 2 =$ _____

    b   Count in 3s for 4 steps is $4 \times 3 =$ _____

    c   Count in 4s for 4 steps is $4 \times 4 =$ _____

    d   Count in 6s for 3 steps is $3 \times 6 =$ _____

Reasoning activity

What do you notice about the numbers when you count in 5s on a number line? What if you started at 1?

111

Kilograms

Try this

Use a balance scale and pairs of objects.

Compare the weight of the objects.

Make a list to show which is heavier and which is lighter.

The book is heavier than the blocks.

Explain

A **kilogram** (kg) is a unit of mass. A packet of sugar is about 1 kg.

Try this

You need some objects to weigh.

Guess the weight of each object.

Is it: • less than 1 kilogram?
  • about 1 kilogram?
  • more than 1 kilogram?

Write the name of the object under the column of your guess.

Less than 1 kilogram	About 1 kilogram	More than 1 kilogram

Decide on how you could weigh the objects to check your answers.

Kilograms and half kilograms

1 kilogram = 1000 grams

$\frac{1}{2}$ kilogram = 500 grams

The short way to write kilogram is kg.

The short way to write grams is g.

1 Does it weigh 1 kilogram or $\frac{1}{2}$ kilogram?

a

b

c

d

Try this

You need:

balance scales different
objects and packages to weigh
1 kg and $\frac{1}{2}$ kg weights

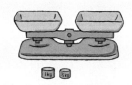

Weigh some different objects. Find objects that weigh the same as 1 kg and
others that weigh about $\frac{1}{2}$ kg.
List them in this table.

1 kilogram	$\frac{1}{2}$ kilogram

Reasoning activity

Work in groups and decide which is the best buy in each pair:

1kg onions for $300 or $\frac{1}{2}$ kg onions for $200

$\frac{1}{2}$ kg rice for $160 or 500g rice for $150

More about kilograms

all these items weigh one kilogram

Try this

Find three things that weigh exactly 1 kg.
Tell a partner what you found.

1 Write whether these items weigh more
than a kilogram (>kg) or less than a
kilogram (<kg).

____ ____ ____ ____ ____

2 Write the total mass of each set.

a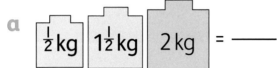

b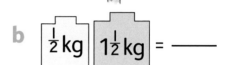

c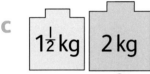

Try this

a Eight tins of sardines weigh 1 kg.
What is the weight in kilograms of 16 tins of sardines?

_____

b A woman buys 2 kg of rice, 3 kg of flour, a box of soda weighing 12 kg and
10 kg of vegetables.
What is the total mass of her purchases?

_____

c A truck carried 97 kg of goods. It delivered 23 kg.
How many kilograms remain?

_____

Reasoning activity

Work in **pairs**, weigh yourselves and calculate these.
How many 10 kg bags of potatoes would weigh about the same as you?

Mass in kilograms

1 Work out the mass of each group of shopping.

a

_____

b

_____

c

_____

d

_____

e

_____

f

_____

g

_____

h

_____

Reasoning activity

Mr Allen's shopping weighs exactly 10kg.
What are the possible contents of his bag?

Grams and kilograms

Explain

These objects all have a mass of about **1 gram** (1 g).

These objects all have a mass of about **1 kilogram** (1 kg).

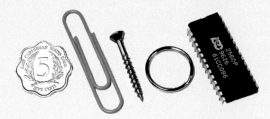

1 Circle the unit you would use to give the mass of these objects.

a   g   kg   b   g   kg   c   g   kg

d   g   kg

e   g   kg

Try this

Use weighing scales to measure the mass of different objects in grams and kilograms.

Which scales do you find the easiest to use?

Is it harder to work out the mass of an object in grams or kilograms?

Measuring mass

Explain

When we measure how heavy something is, we measure its **mass**.
The units for measuring mass are **kilograms** and **grams**.
1000 grams = 1 kilogram
We can write grams and kilograms like this:

one gram   1 g
one kilogram   1 kg

1 Circle the instruments that measure mass.

2 Complete the table.

a	five kilograms	5 kg
b	ten kilograms	_____
c	a hundred grams	_____
d	_____	2 kg
e	twenty-five kilograms	_____
f	_____	90 g

Reasoning activity

Work in pairs using any of the following: rulers, string, books, pencils, glue sticks.
Can you make a simple instrument that can measure mass?

2-D shapes

1 Colour the shapes on the clown.

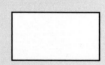

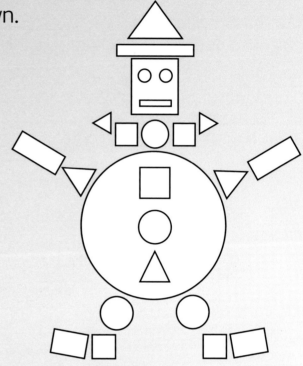

2 How many?

 _____

 _____

 _____

 _____

3 Count the shapes. Fill in the table.

Shape	Number
square	_____
circle	_____
triangle	_____
rectangle	_____

Try this

Which have straight or curved sides?
How many sides does each have?
How many corners does each have?

Reasoning activity

Where can we find shapes like these in daily
life? Draw a poster to show the shapes you find.

Shape and size

1 Match each shape to its name.

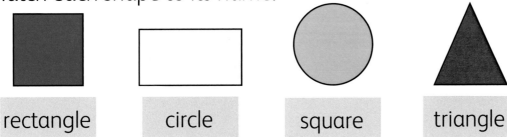

| rectangle | circle | square | triangle |

2 Colour the shape in the right hand column that is the same shape and size as the coloured shape.

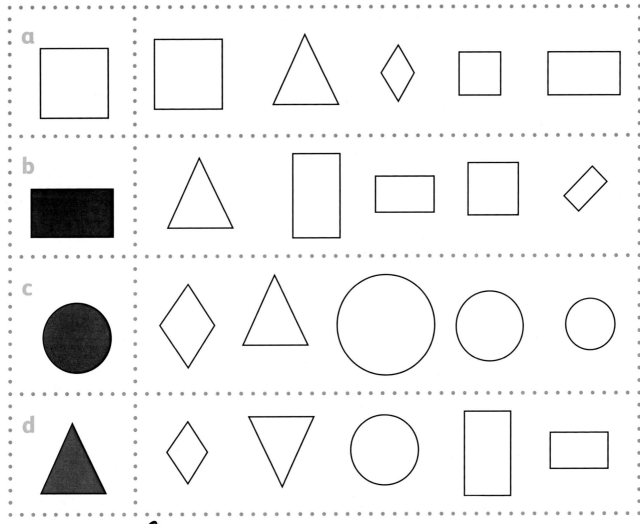

Work in pairs and take turns to choose a shape from this page and describe it. Can your partner find the shape?

Plane shapes

Explain

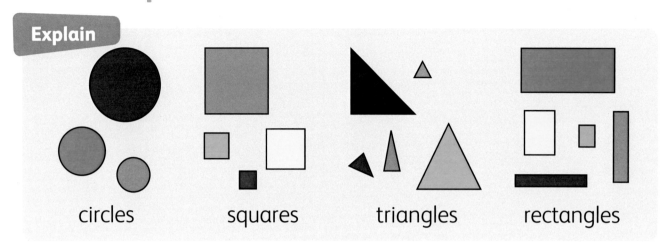

circles   squares   triangles   rectangles

1 **a** Put an ✗ inside each circle below.

   b Colour each square blue.

   c Colour each triangle yellow.

   d Put a tick ✓ inside each rectangle.

2 How many of each shape did you find?
Record your results in the table.

Name of shape	Number found
circle	_____
square	_____
triangle	_____
rectangle	_____
other	_____

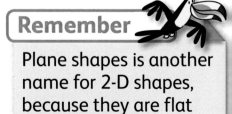

Remember

Plane shapes is another
name for 2-D shapes,
because they are flat
(on one plane).

120

Problems with shapes

1 Circle the shape that does not belong in each set below.
Tell your partner why you have circled this shape.

a

b

c

2 Draw one line to divide these shapes into halves.

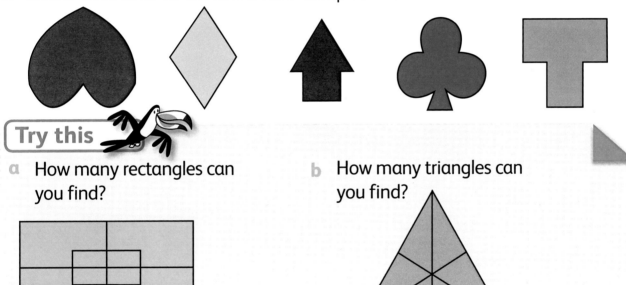

> **Try this**
>
> a How many rectangles can you find?
>
> b How many triangles can you find?
>
>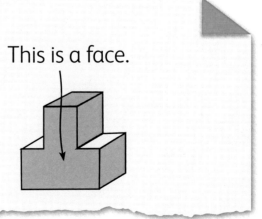

> **Reasoning activity**
>
> Work in pairs and look at this shape.
> Make it from interlocking cubes.
> How many faces can you see?
> How many faces does it have altogether?
>
> This is a face.
>
>

Shapes and ladders

You will need: a die and some counters.

1 Each player takes a turn to throw the die and move their counter.
You do not have to throw a six to start.
The first person home is the winner.

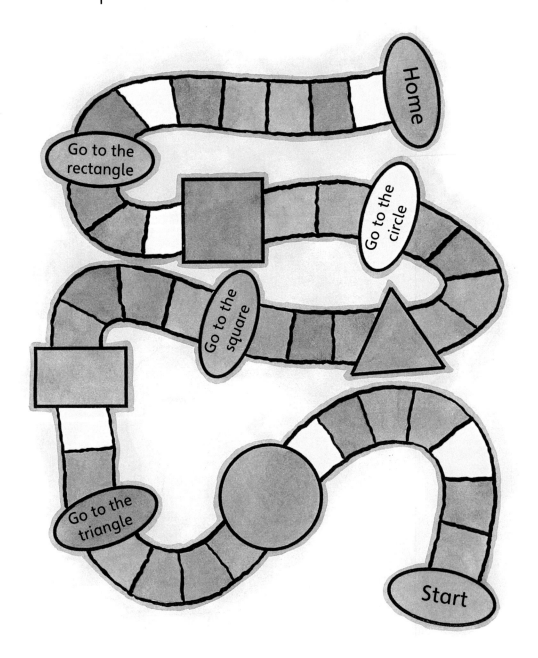

> **Reasoning activity**
>
> Add more instructions to some of the squares so the game is more challenging. You could include 'Move back 3' or 'Miss a turn' for example.

Geometrical shapes in nature

Work in pairs and discuss the patterns and shapes you can see on this page and the next page.

- Is it a plant or an animal, or something else?
- What shapes and colours form the pattern?
- What kinds of lines can you see?
- Are there curves or corners?

 Try this

Nature is full of amazing patterns and shapes. If you can, take pictures of patterns that you see in the grass, flowers, trees and so on and share them with your classmates.

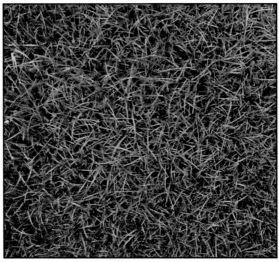

 **Try this**

Where do we use patterns from nature on man made objects?

Assess and review

> I can use arrays to show multiplication facts, compare the weight of different objects using grams and kilograms and describe the properties of 2-D shapes.

1 Use the arrays to help answer these.

3 × 6 = __  4 × 5 = __ 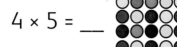 7 × 4 = __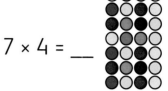

2 Write multiplication sentences for these.

_____ _____ _____

3 Look at the artwork. Which food weighs 1 kg and which weighs 500 kg. Draw your answer in the table.

1 kilogram	½ kilogram

4 Weigh some different items. Find an item that weighs the same as 1 kg and another that weighs about ½ kg. Draw them in this table.

5 List two special properties about each of these shapes.

_____ _____ _____

_____ _____ _____

Extended Project 2

Choosing a sports kit

A school is deciding on a new sports kit and needs help in choosing the colours. They want to have t-shirts, shorts and socks in any choice of red, green or yellow.

- What are all the possible combinations of the three colours and articles of clothing?

Make it easier by looking at the different choices of colour for just the t-shirt and shorts.

Draw, colour and cut out shorts and t-shirts showing each colour:

Put the cut-out clothes together in different ways and record the kit colours.

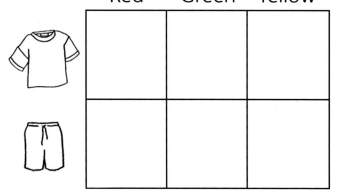

	Red	Green	Yellow

- How many different sports kits with t-shirts and shorts can you make?
- Now include the socks. Can you think of a good method to find all the different possible colours for the sports kit?

Next step

Choose your favourite 5 kit colours. Carry out a class survey of these colours for the sports kit to find the overall favourite. Draw a pictograph or bar chart to show your results.

21 Division

Division: counting the groups

Some boys shared 6 lollipops. They each got 2. How many boys were there?

6 lollipops
3 equal groups.
2 in each group . $6 \div 2 = 3$

1 Circle the groups. Then complete the number sentence.

a 12 sweets. Each friend gets 4 sweets.
How many friends?
____ groups of 4
$12 \div 4 =$ ____

b 16 sweets. Each friend gets 4 sweets.
How many friends?
____ groups of 4
$16 \div 4 =$ ____

c 18 buttons. Each top gets 3 buttons.
How many tops?
____ groups of 3
$18 \div 3 =$ ____

d 15 peas. I put 5 on each plate.
How many plates?
____ groups of 5
$15 \div 5 =$ ____

Remember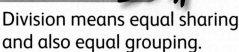

Division means equal sharing
and also equal grouping.

Dividing by grouping

Explain

Division using grouping is a good way of dividing.

The number you are dividing by shows the size of each group.

$20 \div 4 =$ ___

Make groups of 4.

How many groups of 4 make 20?

5 groups of 4 make 20.

$20 \div 4 = 5$

1 Draw your own sets of dots or shapes. Circle to show division.

a $12 \div 2 =$ ____

b $18 \div 3 =$ ____

c $21 \div 7 =$ ____

d $24 \div 6 =$ ____

Try this

Use beans or counters to make groups and work these out.

a $27 \div 3 =$ ____   b $40 \div 5 =$ ____   c $32 \div 8 =$ ____   d $25 \div 5 =$ ____

2 a Michael cut a cake into 15 slices. He wants to put 3 slices on each plate. How many plates does he need?

_____

b Nikki has 48 beads. Each necklace has 8 beads. How many necklaces can she make?

_____

c A baker makes 45 bulla and divides them equally into 5 bags. How many bulla are in each bag?

_____

Dividing with remainders

Divide 10 plums into groups of 4.

$10 \div 4$ = 2 groups and 2 left over

1 Divide equally.
Write the number of groups and the number left over.

a 13 balls

Divide into groups of 2.
$13 \div 2 =$ ___ groups of
balls and ___ left over

b 14 fish

Divide into groups of 5.
$14 \div 5 =$ ___ groups
and ___ left over

c 12 bananas

Divide into groups of 5.
$12 \div 5 =$ _____
and ___ left over

d 18 ants

Divide into groups of 4.
$18 \div 4 =$ _____
and ___ left over

e 21 flies

Divide into groups of 4.
$21 \div 4 =$ _____
and ___ left over

f 12 dragonflies

Divide into groups of 7.
$12 \div 7 =$ _____
and ___ left over

Reasoning activity

Work in pairs using counters. Find numbers that have 1 left over, when
they are grouped in 2s. What do you notice?

Grouping with remainders

1 Use counters, buttons or coins. Make your own groups to help you divide.

24 ÷ 5 = _____
remainder: _____

45 ÷ 6 = _____
remainder: _____

37 ÷ 4 = _____
remainder: _____

19 ÷ 8 = _____
remainder: _____

49 ÷ 9 = _____
remainder: _____

52 ÷ 7 = _____
remainder: _____

50 ÷ 8 = _____
remainder: _____

27 ÷ 6 = _____
remainder: _____

48 ÷ 5 = _____
remainder: _____

33 ÷ 4 = _____
remainder: _____

Try this

a Paul picked 20 oranges. He divided them into bags of 6 oranges. How many full bags did he make?

_____ ÷ _____ = _____

b A case of soda has 32 bottles. The store sells the soda in packs of 5. How many full packs can they sell from a case?

_____ ÷ _____ = _____

The = and ≠ signs

= means **is equal to** $5 + 3 = 4 + 4$

≠ means **is not equal to** $3 + 6 ≠ 5 + 2$

1 Fill in the missing number so that the number sentence is correct. The first one has been done for you.

a $5 + 5 ≠ 11$ $5 + 5 = \underline{10}$

b $7 + 8 ≠ 14$ $7 + 8 = \underline{\quad}$

c $10 - 9 ≠ 2$ $10 - \underline{\quad} = 2$

d $14 - 5 ≠ 10$ $14 - \underline{\quad} = 10$

e $11 + 9 ≠ 18$ $\underline{\quad} + 9 = 18$

f $17 - 4 ≠ 15$ $\underline{\quad} - 4 = 15$

2 Fill in = or ≠ between each pair.

a $3 + 4 \bigcirc 2 + 1$ **b** $9 - 4 \bigcirc 10 - 5$

c $9 + 0 \bigcirc 6 + 3$ **d** $16 - 3 \bigcirc 14 - 4$

e $10 + 3 + 2 \bigcirc 15$ **f** $24 - 1 \bigcirc 30 - 6$

g $11 + 6 \bigcirc 13 + 12$ **h** $48 + 6 \bigcirc 57 - 13$

i $28 + 8 \bigcirc 34 + 8$ **j** $42 - 12 \bigcirc 15 + 5$

Try this

Look back at question 2. For all the answers that had ≠ write the sentences out again. This time use < or > to make them correct.

22 Algebra

Sequences

1 Draw the next three shapes in these patterns.

a

b

c

d

2 Which colour and shape would come next in the sequence?

a

b

c

Repeat patterns

Colours and shapes make good patterns.
How can you work out the next shape and colour for these?

1 Colour the shapes to continue the patterns.

a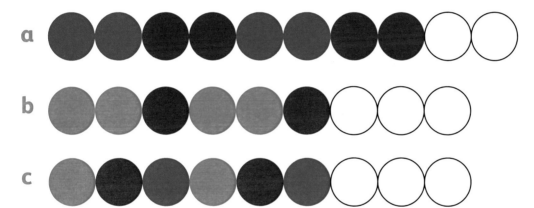

b

c

2 Draw three more shapes on each necklace to continue the pattern.

a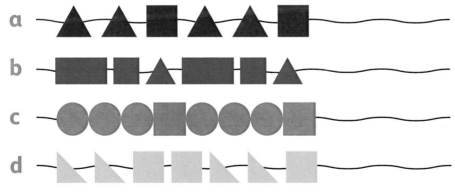

b

c

d

Try this

Draw a necklace and make your own patterns.
Choose two different colours or shapes.

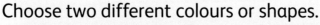

23 Data

Pictographs

A **pictograph** uses a small picture to represent each unit of data. Each marble represents 1 marble. Always ask: What does each picture on the graph show us?

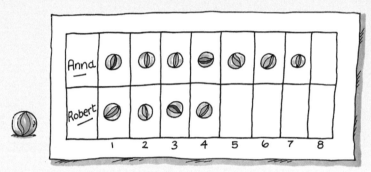

1 Find the answers using the graph.

   a Anna has _____ marbles.

   b Robert has _____ marbles.

   c Anna has _____ more marbles than Robert.

   d The two children have _____ marbles altogether.

   e Robert wins one marble from Anna.

   Who has more? _____ How many more? _____

Reasoning activity

Make up five questions about each of the graphs below.
Ask your friend to answer the questions.

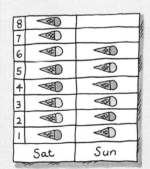

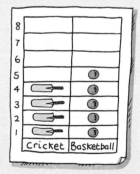

Reading graphs

Fruits we like

 stands for one girl.   stands for one boy.

	mango	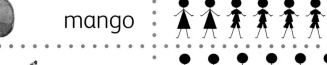
	banana	
	pineapple	
	pear	
	orange	

1 How many children like:

   a mango? _____   pineapple? _____   banana? _____

     orange? _____   pear? _____

   b The most popular fruit is _____.

   c The least popular fruit is _____.

   d How many more children like bananas than like pears? _____

   e Which fruit is liked by as many girls as boys? _____

Reasoning activity

Ask the girls and boys in your class who prefers each of these fruits.
Collect and show your data in a table like the one above.

Remember

Pictographs can be shown horizontally or vertically.
Decide which way round you want to draw your graph.

135

Constructing a pictograph

Agatha sells vegetables at the Ocho Rios market. This table shows how many pumpkins she sold in a week.

Monday	Tuesday	Wednesday	Thursday	Friday
13	11	10	13	18

1 Use the table above to complete these.

　a Agatha sold the most pumpkins on _____ .

　b Agatha sold the fewest pumpkins on _____ .

　c She sold equal numbers of pumpkins on _____ and _____ .

2 Draw your own pictograph to show Agatha's sales.

　 represents 2 pumpkins. The first row has been done.

Monday	🎃 🎃 🎃 🎃 🎃 🎃 (
Tuesday	
Wednesday	
Thursday	
Friday	

Bar graphs

Explain

These children collected shells. A bar graph can show the totals collected to compare amounts.

1 Complete the graph. Colour 1 part of a bar for each shell.

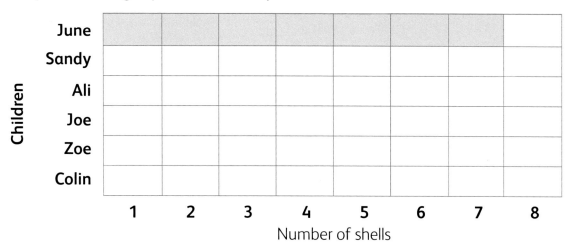

2 Use your graph to find the answers to these.

a _____ collected the most.

b _____ and _____ each found 7 shells.

c _____ shells were found altogether.

d June found _____ more shells than Joe.

e Zoe found _____ fewer shells than Colin.

Reasoning activity

Why do we show data on graphs?

Compare the picture of the children with shells and the graph.

Assess and review

> I can divide by grouping, with and without remainders, continue repeat patterns, construct pictographs and read bar graphs.

1 Use counters. Group them to help you divide.

23 ÷ 5 = _____ remainder _____

19 ÷ 3 = _____ remainder _____

26 ÷ 4 = _____ remainder _____

25 ÷ 2 = _____ remainder _____

2 Solve these problems.

a Joel had 15 mangoes.

He divided them into boxes of 3 mangoes.

How many full boxes did he have?_____

b He also had 28 bananas.

He divided them into bags of 6 bananas.

How many full bags did he have?_____

3 Draw and colour three more shapes in the sequence to continue the pattern.

4 This pictograph shows the sports played by a group of people.

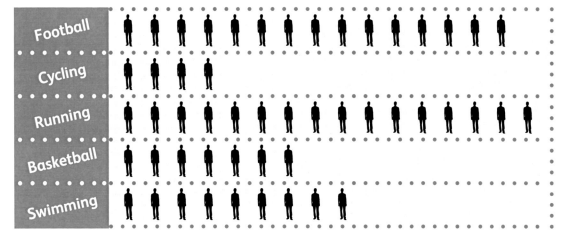

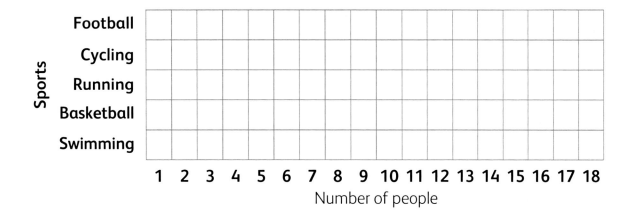 stands for 1 person

How many more people play football than basketball? ___

How many fewer people go cycling than go swimming? ___

5 Draw a bar graph to show the results of the pictograph above.

Sports																		
Football																		
Cycling																		
Running																		
Basketball																		
Swimming																		

1 2 3 4 5 6 7 8 9 10 11 12 13 14 15 16 17 18
Number of people

24 More fractions

Unit fractions

This shows **one half**.

$\dfrac{1}{2}$

1 part is shaded
2 equal parts

This shows **one quarter**.

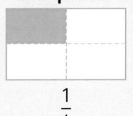

$\dfrac{1}{4}$

1 part is shaded
4 equal parts

1 Shade one part of each shape below.

2 Write the fraction shaded.

a _____

b _____

c _____

d 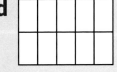 _____

e _____

f  _____

g 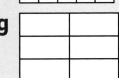 _____

h _____

i 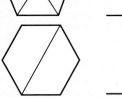 _____

Reasoning activity

How could we write the fraction if more than one part was shaded?

Remember

The denominator (the number at the bottom) tells us how many equal parts the whole has been divided into. The numerator (the number on top) tells us how many of the equal parts are used. A unit fraction has 1 as the numerator.

How many parts?

1 How many parts have been coloured in each set?
Write the fraction. The first one has been done.

a

1 of 2 equal parts = $\frac{1}{2}$ 2 of 2 parts = $\frac{2}{2}$

b

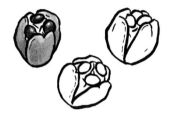 

$\frac{\boxed{}}{3}$ $\frac{\boxed{}}{3}$ $\frac{\boxed{}}{3}$

c

$\frac{\boxed{}}{4}$ $\frac{\boxed{}}{4}$ $\frac{\boxed{}}{4}$ $\frac{\boxed{}}{4}$

2 Write the fraction of each set that is coloured.

a    **b**    **c**    **d**

_____   _____   _____   _____

Fractions of a set

Here are 8 trees. 3 out of the 8 trees have fruit.

$\frac{3}{8}$ of the trees have fruit.

1 _____ out of _____ boats have sails. $\boxed{}$ of the boats have sails.

2 _____ out of _____ fruit are mangoes. $\boxed{}$ of the fruit are mangoes.

3 _____ out of _____ fruit are strawberries. $\boxed{}$ of the fruit are strawberries.

4 _____ out of _____ elephants are pink. $\boxed{}$ of the elephants are pink.

5 _____ out of _____ cows have bells. $\boxed{}$ of the cows have bells.

Reasoning activity

Work in groups and try and draw these 8 fish.

$\frac{3}{8}$ are big, $\frac{5}{8}$ have black spots, $\frac{7}{8}$ are orange.

Adding and subtracting fractions

Explain

The picture shows that $\frac{1}{7} + \frac{3}{7} = \frac{4}{7}$.

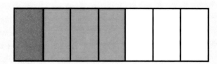

1 Write a number sentence and add the different coloured fractions shown on each diagram.

a

$\boxed{} + \boxed{} = \boxed{}$

b

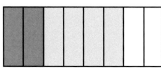

$\boxed{} + \boxed{} = \boxed{}$

c

$\boxed{} + \boxed{} = \boxed{}$

d

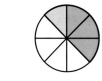

$\boxed{} + \boxed{} = \boxed{}$

2 Complete these.

a $\frac{2}{3} + \frac{1}{3} = \boxed{}$

b $\frac{2}{7} + \frac{3}{7} = \boxed{}$

c $\frac{2}{3} + \frac{3}{3} = \boxed{}$

d $\frac{4}{5} - \frac{1}{5} = \boxed{}$

e $\frac{7}{8} - \frac{5}{8} = \boxed{}$

f $\frac{3}{4} - \frac{1}{4} = \boxed{}$

Reasoning activity

When do we use fractions in everyday life? **Work in groups.**

3 Fill in >, < or =. Draw diagrams to help you if you need to.

a $\frac{2}{7} \bigcirc \frac{5}{7}$

b $\frac{1}{3} \bigcirc \frac{2}{6}$

c $\frac{2}{5} \bigcirc \frac{4}{10}$

d $\frac{3}{5} \bigcirc \frac{1}{5}$

e $\frac{3}{7} \bigcirc \frac{4}{7}$

f $\frac{1}{2} \bigcirc \frac{4}{8}$

Remember

When denominators are the same, addition and subtraction of fractions just means adding or subtracting the numerators (top numbers).

25 Temperature

Temperature

Temperature tells you how hot or cold something is.

A **thermometer** is used to measure how hot or how cold.

1 Write **hot** or **cold** for each of these.

a

b

c

d

e

f

Try this

Find out where in the world the temperature is very cold and where it is very hot. Look at an atlas to show the countries.

Using a thermometer

Try this

Use a thermometer. Measure the temperature in the classroom every morning and afternoon for 10 days. Complete the table below.

	Day 1	Day 2	Day 3	Day 4	Day 5
Date					
Morning					
Afternoon					
	Day 6	Day 7	Day 8	Day 9	Day 10
Date					
Morning					
Afternoon					

The highest temperature was _____.

The lowest temperature was _____.

Reasoning activity

Was the temperature mostly warmer in the morning or in the afternoon? Why do you think that happened?

1 Compare temperatures. Write **warmer** or **cooler** under the second picture in each pair.

a

_____

b

_____

Which unit?

Reasoning activity

We use different units to measure length, mass and capacity.

Sort these so they are grouped together correctly.

When would you use each unit?

meter   centimetre

litre   kilogram

gram

mililitre   kiolmetre

1 For each object, circle the correct unit.

a

height of a flower

cm   km   g

b

mass of an apple

cm   g   cups

c

amount of water
a bottle holds

l   g   cm

d

height of a tree

m   km   kg

e

how cold a drink is

°c   kg   km

f

length of a pencil

km   m   cm

g

distance between
two cities

cm   m   km

h

mass of a dozen
apples

km   kg   g

Symmetry

line of symmetry

A **line of symmetry** divides a shape into parts that are the same shape and size, and fit together exactly when you fold along the line.

1 All the shapes below have a line of symmetry.
Complete and colour the shapes.

a

b

c

d

e

f

Try this

Trace and cut out each shape. Fold along the dotted line to check whether it is a line of symmetry.

Reasoning activity

Work in pairs and look for symmetry on your body.
Is your face symmetrical?
Is your body symmetrical?
What about the side view of your face or body?
Is a hand or a foot symmetrical?

Symmetrical patterns

Try this

Symmetrical patterns can be folded into 2 equal parts.
Let's explore blotting.

Try your own blot pattern. What do you notice about the pattern?

1 Look at the patterns. Tick the ones that are symmetrical.

a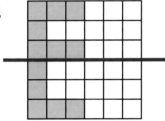

b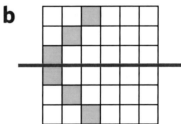

c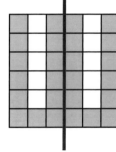

d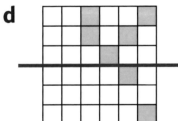

e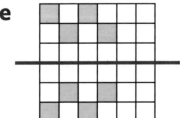

f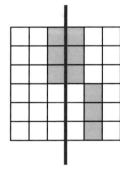

Reasoning activity

Now create your own symmetrical patterns.

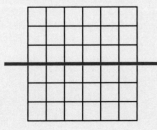 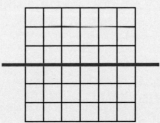 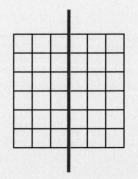

Symmetrical shapes

1 Draw as many lines of symmetry as you can find in each shape.

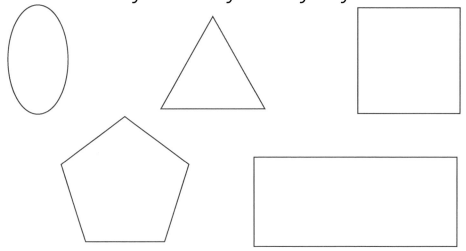

2 Look around the classroom. Make a list of the symmetrical shapes you can see.

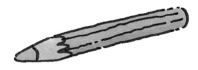

Reasoning activity

'Triangles have a line of symmetry.'
Is this always true, sometimes true or never true?
How could you prove it? Talk about this **in groups**.

27 More algebra

Missing numbers

addend + addend = sum   4 + 5 = 9
   sum − addend = addend   9 − 4 = 5

Sum	
Addend	Addend

1 Fill in the missing addend or sum. Draw bar models to help you.

a ____ + 14 = 30   **b** 37 − 17 = ____   **c** 31 − ____ = 20

d 56 − 23 = ____   **e** 22 + ____ = 49   **f** ____ − 40 = 39

2 Fill in the missing numbers.

31	32		34	35		37	38		40
41		43		45			48	49	
	52	53	54		56		58		60

What do you notice?

3 What are the missing digits?

a ☐☐
     +   7
    ──────
     2 9

b 6 7
     − ☐☐
    ──────
       1 3

c ☐☐
     − 2 5
    ──────
       1 6

What could the missing numbers be?
____ + ____ = 18
How many different additions can you make that total 18?

Algebra problems

1 a Paula has 5 mangoes. Her friend gave her ☐ more mangoes. Paula now has 9 mangoes.

How many mangoes did her friend give her? ____

b On your teacher's desk there were ☐ sticks of chalk. The principal gave her 7 more sticks of chalk. She now has 13 sticks of chalk.

How many sticks of chalk were on her desk at the start? ____

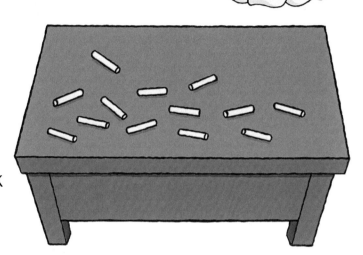

c 8 was added to a number ☐.

If the total is now 23, what was the missing number? ____

2 a A farmer had ☐ goats on his farm.

Thieves broke in and stole 8 goats, and left him with 6 goats.

How many goats did he have at the start? ____

b There are ☐ teachers at a school. There are 6 grades.

Each grade has 3 teachers.

How many teachers are there? ____

> **Reasoning activity**
>
> There are 20 flowers in a vase. *N* flowers are yellow.
> 12 flowers are red.
> What is the value of *N* ?

Assess and review

I can describe fractions of shapes and objects, add and subtract fractions, use a thermometer to read the temperature, identify symmetrical shapes and work out missing numbers in sentences.

1 Shade one part of each of these. Write the fraction shaded.

2 Write the fraction of each set that is red.

_____   _____   _____

3 Draw lines to join each thermometer to the correct picture.

4 Tick the shapes that are symmetrical.

Draw your own symmetrical shape with a line of symmetry.

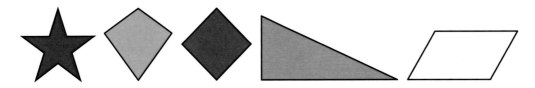

5 Write the missing numbers.

__ + 12 = 40   15 + __ = 36   __ + 60 = 100

__ − 20 = 55   18 + __ = 48   __ − 40 = 30

28 Types of fraction

Fractions of a set

Explain

Here is a set of 8 pans.
Divide it into 2 equal sets.
Each set has 4 pans.

$\frac{1}{2}$ of 8 = 4

Here is a set of 20 spoons.
Divide it into 4 equal sets.
Each set has 5 spoons.

$\frac{1}{4}$ of 20 = 5

1 Circle the sets. Then work out the answer.

a

$\frac{1}{2}$ of 10 = ____

b

$\frac{1}{4}$ of 12 = ____

c

$\frac{1}{3}$ of 6 = ____

d

$\frac{1}{2}$ of 14 = ____

e

$\frac{1}{4}$ of 24 = ____

f

$\frac{1}{5}$ of 20 = ____

g

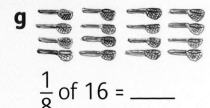

$\frac{1}{8}$ of 16 = ____

h

$\frac{1}{3}$ of 12 = ____

153

Fractions equal to a whole

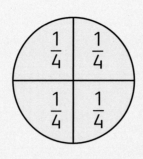

$\frac{2}{2}$ = 1 whole $\frac{4}{4}$ = 1 whole $\frac{3}{3}$ = 1 whole

1 Count the parts of each shape below.

2 Write how many parts are shaded as a fraction.

a

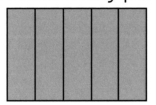

_____ = 1 whole

b

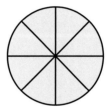

_____ = 1 whole

c

_____ = 1 whole

d

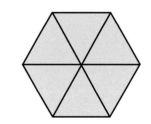

_____ = 1 whole

e

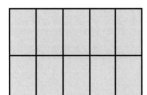

_____ = 1 whole

f

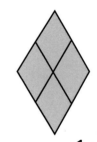

_____ = 1 whole

Reasoning activity

Three pizzas of the same size are sliced in different ways:

Halves   Thirds   Quarters

How many slices are there altogether?

Are they equal sizes? How can you prove it?

How many halves and quarters?

1 Count how many halves are in each.

a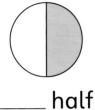

b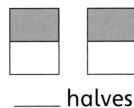

c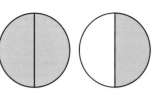

_____ half   _____ halves   _____ halves

d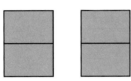

e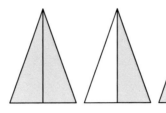

_____ halves   _____ halves

Reasoning activity

What do you notice?

2 Count and write the numbers of quarters in each of these patterns.

a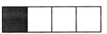

_____ quarters

b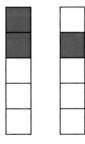

_____ quarters

c
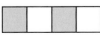
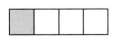

_____ quarters

d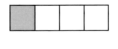

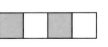

_____ quarters

155

29 Data and probability

Measuring

Try this

Work in a group of six.

a Use a tape measure to measure each other's arm lengths in centimetres (cm).

b Fill in the data in the table.

Name	Arm length

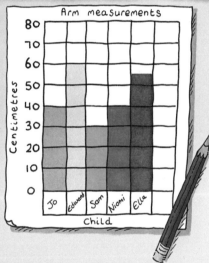

1 Use the graph to answer these questions.

a Who had the biggest arm measurement? _____

b Who had the smallest arm measurement? _____

c Which children have the same arm length? _____

d What is your arm measurement? _____
   Fill it in on the graph.

Try this

Use your results to compare the arm lengths of your group. Draw a bar graph to show the results.

Possible events

Explain

Certain means it will surely happen.

Impossible means it cannot possibly happen.

Maybe means it could happen.

Tick **certain**, **impossible** or **maybe** for each event.

	Certain	Impossible	Maybe
I will fly to the moon tomorrow.			
The sun will rise tomorrow morning.			
I will eat something tomorrow.			
I will see the stars tonight.			
It will be cloudy tomorrow.			
It will rain tomorrow.			
A tree will talk to me today.			

Reasoning activity

In groups discuss the terms *certain, impossible* and
maybe. Take turns to say a statement using certain, impossible and maybe.

157

Certain, impossible and maybe

Explain

I have these socks in a drawer:

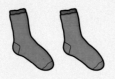

2 blue socks

2 green socks

I pull out 2 socks

Could they be:		Certain	Impossible	Maybe
1 red sock and 1 blue sock?			✓	
1 blue sock and 1 green sock?				✓

1 I have these socks in a drawer:

a I pull out one sock.

Could it be:	Certain	Impossible	Maybe
red?			
green?			
yellow?			

b It is certain that I will get either a _____ or a _____ sock.

c It is impossible that I will get a _____ sock.

2 I have these coins in a purse:
I pull out three coins.

a It is (certain / possible) that they will be a $1, $20 and $5 coin.

b It is (certain / possible / impossible) that they will be three $5 coins.

Assess and review

> I can work out fractions of a set and use certain, impossible or maybe to describe whether an event will happen.

1 Circle the sets and answer these.

$\frac{1}{3}$ of 15 = ____

$\frac{1}{8}$ of 16 = ____

$\frac{1}{6}$ of 12 = ____

$\frac{1}{5}$ of 20 = ____

2 Complete these.

1 whole = ____ halves $1 = \frac{\Box}{2}$

1 whole = ____ quarters $1 = \frac{\Box}{4}$

1 whole = ____ thirds $1 = \frac{\Box}{3}$

3 I have these coins in a purse. I take out one coin.

Could it be:	Certain	Impossible	Maybe
a $5 coin?			
a $10 coin?			
a coin worth more than $2?			

159

Extended Project 3

A day at the zoo

Alicia and her family are visiting the zoo. Help her solve these different problems.

1 How many zebras are in the barn?

Work as a group and read the clues.

Sort out the clues. Which are important ones? Use counters to help you work it out.

> The zoo has 32 zebras altogether.

> Some of the zebras are in the barn or by the pond.

> The barn holds fewer than 10 zebras.

> Half of the zebras are outside on the grass.

> 9 zebras are by the pond.

> The zookeeper kept some of the zebras in the barn.

> The zebras are kept in three different places.

2 The Big Cat Centre is an interesting shape with four different enclosures.

How many different routes are there to walk from the entrance to the exit, without walking back at any point?

How can you prove you have found all the possible routes?

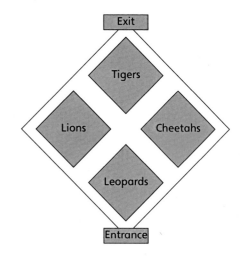

3 The birds of prey are kept in 5 large enclosures like this.

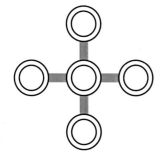

There are 15 birds altogether.

Can you arrange the birds so there are 10 birds in each line?

What if there were more birds. Is it still possible to make lines of 10 birds?

Next step

Think of other animals you would see at a zoo. Design your own zoo. Work out how many different areas you would need. How would you group the animals?

Draw a picture to show your zoo. How many animals have you got altogether?